A DICTIONARY
OF
SPECIAL EDUCATION TERMS

A DICTIONARY OF

SPECIAL EDUCATION

TERMS

By

BYRON C. MOORE, Ed.D.
Arizona State University
Tempe, Arizona

WILLARD ABRAHAM, Ph.D.
Arizona State University
Tempe, Arizona

CLARENCE R. LAING, M.D.
Good Samaritan Hospital
Phoenix, Arizona

With a Foreword by
Samuel A. Kirk

CHARLES C THOMAS • PUBLISHER
Springfield • Illinois • U.S.A.

Published and Distributed Throughout the World by
CHARLES C THOMAS • PUBLISHER
Bannerstone House
301-327 East Lawrence Avenue, Springfield, Illinois, U.S.A.

©*1980, by* CHARLES C THOMAS • PUBLISHER
ISBN 0-398-04009-5
Library of Congress Catalog Card Number: 79-23015

Library of Congress Cataloging in Publication Data

Moore, Byron C
    A dictionary of special education terms.

    1. Exceptional children—Education—Dictionaries. I. Abraham, Willard, joint author.
II. Laing, Clarence R., joint author. III. Title.
LB15.M63   371.9'03   79-23015
ISBN 0-398-04009-5

Printed in the United States of America
M-3

FOREWORD

In his book on pragmatism written during the early part of this century, William James gave an example that emphasizes the importance of adequate definitions of words. He was reminded of a heated argument at a picnic. At this gathering, a man was walking around a tree and a squirrel was going around the same tree, keeping himself on the opposite side. One group of onlookers alleged that the man was going around the squirrel, while another group insisted that the man was *not* going around the squirrel. They asked William James to help them solve the argument.

The solution to the argument, said William James, depends on your definition of "around." If by "around" you mean going from the front of an object, to the side, to the back, to the other side, and then returning to the front, the man was not going around the squirrel. If, on the other hand, you define "around" as going from the North, to the East, to the South, to the West, and then to the North, then the man was going around the squirrel. The settlement of the argument, said philosopher James, depends on the definition of the word "around."

If William James' emphasis on definitions of words is correct, and I am sure it is, I am pleased to write a foreword to *A Dictionary of Special Education Terms.* I think that a compilation of many terms now being used in special education requires a baseline of definitions so that communication is more consistent and controversies resolved.

It is customary with current textbooks that glossaries be included. These, however, are usually limited to some of the words in the text and are not inclusive.

The authors of this dictionary have spent a great deal of time defining and refining the concepts that are included in each word. If we were to clearly agree on definitions of terms, many of our current disagreements, controversies, and concepts could be clarified. It is hoped that this compilation of definitions will contribute to clearer concepts and a better understanding of the education of exceptional children.

Samuel A. Kirk

INTRODUCTION

Special education touches upon many different professional disciplines as well as diverse categories of handicapped conditions. The major areas with which this dictionary is concerned include mental retardation, emotional handicaps, hearing, vision and learning disability, speech, physical handicaps and giftedness. The terminology included herein is judged to be the most frequently used in the field of special education today. Word usage was determined by examining the indices, glossaries and tables of contents of the major special education textbooks currently on the market. The authors, with backgrounds in special education, psychology and medicine, are thoroughly convinced that the education and management of handicapped individuals requires the utmost in cooperation between many different disciplines.

Mental retardation, for example, is a genetic, pediatric, social, psychological, and educational problem . . . to name just a few disciplines with a vested interest. In order for representatives of these disciplines to cooperate in the best interests of their client-patient-student, they must understand each other's language. To meet the varying needs of all participants in the special education picture required this dictionary's compilers to restrict emphasis to definitions primarily related to exceptional children from an educational point of view. The field of special education is in a state of ferment, and so are the people in it. New concepts, new techniques and new terms seem to submerge us, and we need all the help we can get to clarify what we and others mean. Semantics has always been troublesome, but at no time in the short history of special education has there been so much misunderstanding. As a wise man once said, "If something can be misunderstood, it will be."

The special education orbit has been expanded considerably through the passage of The Education for All Handicapped Children Act (Public Law 94-142) for now all regular classroom teachers and school administrators are literally involved in our area of concern. They too must be up-to-date on the changing terminology and concepts. The broadening range of children under the umbrella of education (including the multiply and severely handicapped), for example, alerts us to the fact that special education is now everyone's business and everyone's responsibility.

A pronunciation key and guide has been included to assist students with word sounds. The authors selected and were granted permission to use a Scott, Foresman and Company pronunciation guide from *Writer's Guide and Index to English* by Porter G. Perrin. In each case, only one pronunciation has been offered—that which was deemed most common in usage.

ACKNOWLEDGMENTS

It is doubtful that anyone ever compiled a dictionary, or any book for that matter, without a lot of assistance and encouragement from others. The authors are no exception. In our case, graduate students Ann Rispoli, Lenore Angichiodo and Komonporn Veckchalikanon spent hours searching out glossaries, indices and other vocabulary sources as the authors built up the card files for this book. Eve Mantel who typed every syllable of the text deserves a special award. She had to learn to type a special script in order to do the pronunciation guide. And finally, Susan Moore, coauthor and editorial assistant in all the senior author's more recent works, has our special thanks for her suggestions, constructive criticism and labor.

> Byron C. Moore
> Willard Abraham
> Clarence R. Laing

A DICTIONARY
OF
SPECIAL EDUCATION TERMS

PRONUNCIATION KEY

a   apple \ap´əl\, fact \fakt\
ā   age \āj\, say \sā\
ä   far \fär\, fall \fäl\
ăr   care \kăr\, fair \făr\
b   back \bak\, robber \rob´ėr\
ch   child \chīld\, church \chėrch\
d   did \did\, doctor \dok´tėr\
e   bet \bet\, effect \ə fekt´\
ē   equal \ē kwəl\, see \sē\
ėr   bird \bėrd\, term \tėrm\
ēr   ear \ēr\, here \hēr\
f   fat \fat\, stuff \stuf\
g   go \gō\, baggage \bag´ij\
h   hotel \hō tel´\, boyhood \boi´hůd\
i   if \if\, sister \sis´tėr\
ī   ice \īs\, buy \bī\
j   jam \jam\, edge \ej\
k   king \king\, car \kär\
l   life \līf\, silly \sil´ē\, fill \fil\
m   am \am\, meet \mēt\
n   note \nōt\, inner \in´ėr\
o   rock \rok\, stop \stop\
ô   ball \bôl\, bought \bôt\, caught \kôt\
ôr   for \fôr\, court \kôrt\
oi   voice \vois\, boy \boi\
ou   house \hous\, cow \kou
p   paper \pā´pėr\, cap \kap\
r   reach \rēch\, try \tri\
s   say \sā\, listen \lis´ən\, yes \yes\
sh   she \shē\, rush \rush\
t   tie \tī\, sit \sit\, kitten \kit´ən\
th   thin \thin\, both \bōth\, bath \bath\
ŧh   that \ŧhat\, bother \boŧh´ėr\
u   cup \kup\, butter \but´ėr\
ů   book \bůk\, put \půt\
ü   tool \tül\, rule \rül\, move \müv\
ū   useful \ūs´fəl\, music \mū´zik\
ûr   sure \shûr\, demur \di mûr´\
v   very \văr´ē\, save \sāv\
w   will \wil\, won´t \wōnt\
y   young \yung\, yellow \yel´ō\
z   zero \zēr´ō\, breeze \brēz\
zh   measure \mezh´ėr\, rouge \rüzh\
ə   sofa \sō´fə\, elephant \el´ə fənt\

The above pronunciation key was adapted from *Writer's Guide and Index to English,* Fourth Edition, by Porter G. Perrin. Copyright © 1965 by Scott, Foresman and Company, Reprinted by permission.

3

A **abacus** \ab´ə kəs\ a device employed in performing arithmetic functions that is commonly used with the blind

abalienated \ab˝ āl yə nā´təd\ psychotic

abandon \ə ban´dən\ withdraw or give up when faced with danger, fear or uncertainty

abase \ə bās´\ humiliate, demean, humble

abash \ə bash´\ embarrass; make ashamed and uneasy

abasia \ə bā´zhə\ difficulty in walking due to motor incoordination

abasia-astasia \ə bā´zhə-ə stā´zhə\ gait and stance abnormalities of psychiatric origin

abatement \ə bāt´mənt\ decrease in the severity of pain, or of a disease or condition

abduction \ab duk´shən\ motion of the limbs directed away from midline of the body

abductor \ab duk´tôr\ muscle that moves a limb away from the midline of the body

aberrant \ab ėr´ənt\ deviating from the usual, typical, current or normal

aberration \ab˝ėr ā´shən\ deviation from the normal or usual; irregularity of chromosome distribution during cell division

ability \ə bil´i tē\ competence, proficiency or skill; specific form of intelligence, such as motor or verbal

abiosis \ab˝ē ō´sis\ absence of life

abiotrophy \ab˝ē o´trə fē\ breakdown of tissues; premature loss of vitality or degeneration of tissues and cells with consequent loss of endurance and resistance

ablaction \ab lak´shən\ weaning; cessation of milk secretion

ablation \ab lā´shən\ surgical removal of diseased organs, tissue or growths from the body

ablepharia \ab˝lə fär´ē ə\ congenital reduction or absence of eyelids; ablephary

ablepsia \ab lep´sē ə\ loss of or lack of sight

ablutomania \ə blü˝tə mā´nē ə\ compulsive bathing, washing or cleaning one's self

abnormal \ab nôr´məl\ deviating from the usual or customary

abnormality \ab˝nôr mal´ə tē\ deformity; condition that deviates from the usual or customary

abocclusion \ab˝ə klü˝zhən\ improper contact or lack of contact between upper and lower teeth

aborigine \ab˝ ə rij´ə nē\ earliest known inhabitant of a region or territory

aborticide \ä bōr´tə sīd\ substance that destroys fetal life; the act of destroying fetal life

abortion \ä bôr´shən\ premature separation of the fetus from the uterus, occurring as a result of either internal or external circumstances; termination of specific physical actions prematurely

abrachia \ə brā´kē ə\ congenital absence of the arms

abreaction \ab˝ rē ak´shən\ release of repressed or forgotten emotion through speech or action

abscess \ab´ses\ infection; a localized collection of pus in any part of the body

abscissa \ab sis´ə\ horizontal reference line of a two-dimensioned chart

absence \ab´səns\ being without, away; temporary loss of consciousness

absentminded \ab˝´sənt mīn´dəd\ mental state in which one is preoccupied with thought and unaware of environmental circumstances

absinthism \ab´sin thiz˝əm\ mental or nervous disorder due to excessive use of alcohol, especially absinthe

absorption \ab sôrp´shən\ process of taking fluids or other substances through the skin, mucous membranes or vessels

abstract \ab´strakt\ conceived apart from concrete or functional reality

abstract reasoning \ab´strakt rē´sən ing\ ability to derive meanings from symbols

abulia \ə bū´lē ə\ inability to make a decision; hesitation

abuse \ ə būz\ mistreat; misuse; oppress; annoy; hurt

academic achievement \ak˝ə dem´ik ə chēv´mənt\ scholastic level attained

acalculia \ā´´kal kü´lē ə\ unable to do simple arithmetic or solve mathematical problems

acampsia \ā kamp´sē ə\ inability to bend; inflexibility of a limb; rigidity; abnormal immobility

acanthesthesia \ā´´kan thəs thēz´ē ə\ sensation or prickly feeling of pins and needles

acanthoma \ak´´an thō´mə\ benign skin tumor

acanthosis \ak´´an thō´ sis\ skin disease marked by increased thickness of skin accompanied by warts

acapnia \ə kap´nē ə\ less than the normal amount of carbon dioxide in blood or tissues

acardia \ā kär´dē ə\ born without a heart

acarophobia \ak´´ ə rə fō´bē ə\ morbid fear of small things; fear of infestation, small parasites or microorganisms

acarpous \ā kär´pəs\ bearing no fruit; sterile

acatalepsy \ā kat´´ ə lep´sē\ mental deficiency; inability to understand

acatamathesia \ā kat´´ə mə thē´zhə\ inability to understand spoken words

acataphasia \ā kat´´ə fā´zhə\ inability to express thought orally in a coherent manner

acathexia \ak´´ə thek´sē ə\ inability of the body to control normal excretions and secretions

acceleration \ak sel´´ ə rā´ shən\ the practice of moving gifted children forward in school according to achievement level rather than age-grade level

accent \ak´sent\ emphasis given to a syllable or word in oral language; a particular pronunciation characteristic of a specific group or region

acceptance \ak sep´təns\ the feeling of being understood and liked

acclimation \ak´´li mā´shən\ becoming adjusted to a new environment or situation

accommodation \ə kom´´ə dā´shən\ the ability of the eye to automatically change focus from object to object located at differing distances

accouchement \a küsh mon´\ childbirth

acculturation \ə kul´´chə rā´shən\ the adoption of ideologies, behaviors and beliefs of another group

acedia \ə sē´dē ə\ melancholia; mental state characterized by depression and apathy

acenesthesia \ā´´sen es thē´zhə\ below normal perception of one's body

acentric \ā sen´trik\ not centrally located; used especially in connection with positioning of centromeres within chromosomes

acephalus \ā sef´ə ləs\ a condition in which a fetus does not develop a head

acephaly \ā sef´ə lē\ condition in which a fetus is born without a head

acerbity \ə sėr´bi tē\ harshness of temper or words; irritability

acetabulum \as´´ə tab´ū lum\ cup-shaped depression on the side of hip bone that holds the head of the femur

acetone \as´ ə tōn\ a colorless liquid excreted in above normal quantities in diabetic urine; (CH_3CO-CH_3)

acheiria \ə kī´rē ə\ congenital absence of one or both hands

achievement test \ ə chēv´mənt test\ evaluation of academic performance

Achilles tendon \ə kil´ēz ten´dən\ tendon connecting heel bone to calf muscles

achiria \ə kī´rē ə\ congenital absence of one or both hands; acheiria

achloropsia \ā´´klō rōp´ sē ə\ green color blindness

achondrogenesis \ə kon´´ drō jen´ə sis\ a form of dwarfism involving severe shortness of the limbs and unmineralized vertebrae

achondroplasia \ə kon´´drō plā zhə\ hereditary type of dwarfism characterized by a normal-sized body accompanied by shortened arms and legs and craniofacial abnormalities

achromasia \ak″ro mā zhə\ absence of normal skin pigmentation as in albinism

achromate \ak′rō māt\ totally color-blind person

achromatic \ak″rō mat′ik\ refers to defect in ability to discriminate colors

achromatism \ā krō′mə tiz″əm\ defect in ability to discriminate colors

acid \as′id\ a sour tasting chemical that has the capability for neutralizing alkalis; a slang term for lysergic acid diethylamide (LSD)

acidemia \as″i dē′mē ə\ condition of high level of acid in the blood

acmesthesia \ak″məs thē″ zhə\ inability to feel pain

acne \ak′nē\ oily skin inflammation of the face, back or chest

acne vulgaris \ak′nē vul gär′ is\ inflammation involving the oil glands and hair follicles of the skin and occurring most often in adolescents

acoasma \ak′o az″mə\ auditory hallucination

aconuresis \ak″ə nū rē′sis\ involuntary urination

acoria \ə kôr′ē ə\ hunger sensation that is not relieved by eating

acoumeter \ə kü′mə tėr\ instrument used to determine hearing acuteness

acousma \ə küs′mə\ nonverbal, subjective sounds caused by disturbances in the middle or inner ear; auditory hallucination

acousmatagnosis \ə küs″mat əg nō′sis\ inability to understand what is spoken due to mental disorder

acousticophobia \ə kü″sti kō fō′bē ə\ morbid fear of sounds

acoustics \ə küs′ tiks\ pertaining to sound or sense of hearing; science of sounds

acquired \ə kwīrd′\ of environmental rather than hereditary origin

acrasia \ə krā′zhə\ neurotically self-indulgent and intemperate; lacking self-control

acratia \ə krā′shə\ weakness; loss of strength; impotence

acrid \ak′rid\ pungent; burning; bitter; sharp; irritating

acrimony \ak′ri mō′nē\ harshness of manner or speech

acroagnosis \ak″rō ag nō′sis\ lack of sensation in one's limbs

acrocentric \ak′rō sen′trik\ type of chromosome in which the centromere is located near one end

acrocephaly \ak″rō sef′ə lē\ cranial abnormality characterized by a tall head and mental retardation; oxycephaly

acrocephalosyndactyly \ak″rō sef″ə lō sin dak′tə lē\ congenital condition characterized by a tall, deformed head accompanied by webbing of the hands and feet and retardation

acroedema \ak″rō ə dē′mə\ chronic swelling of the hands and feet

acromania \ak″rō mā′nē ə\ mental disturbance marked by hyperactivity

acromegaly \ak″rō meg′ə lē\ a chronic disease characterized by enlargement of the fingers, toes, nose and jaw due to hormone overproduction

acromicria \ak″rō mik′rē ə\ congenital smallness of the extremities; Down's syndrome

acroparesthesia \ak″rō pär″əs thē′ zhə\ intense tingling or numbness of the hands or feet occurring following sleep

acrophobia \ak″rō fō′bē ə\ chronic, unreasonable fear of being in high places.

acting out \ak′ting out\ overt expression of emotion rather than controlling emotion through suppression or other means

actinogen \ak″tin′ō jən\ radiation-producing material; radioactive element

active hostility \ak′tiv hos til′i tē\ behavior of angry person who wishes to hurt others by actions or words

actualize \ak′chü ə līz\ to make actual or real

acuity \ə kū′i tē\ clearness or sharpness of the senses

acute \ə kūt′\ sudden and severe phases of disease

acyanoblepsia \ə sī″ə nō blep′ sē ə\

color blindness based on inability to discern blue colors

adacrya \ə dak´rē ə\ inability to cry

adactylia \ə dak til´ē ə\ absence of fingers or toes; adactyly

adaptation \ad´´ap tā´shən\ ability to adjust in structure or behavior; in reference to vision, refers to power of the eye to adjust to varying light intensities

adaptation effect \ad´´ap tā´shən ə fekt´\ the improvement of speech quality with practice; decrease in stuttering by successive repeating of the same sentence

adapted abacus \ə dap´təd ab´ə kus\ instrument employed in calculating that is designed for use by the blind

adaptive behavior \ə dap´tiv bē hāv´yėr\ actions of an individual that attempt to meet the standards of responsibility and independence required for his or her age and social group

addict \ad´ikt\ person habituated to the use of alcohol or narcotic drugs

addiction \ə dik´shən\ habituation

Addison's disease \ad´i sunz di zēz´\ adrenal deficiency with symptoms of weakness, nausea, weight loss and digestive disorders

additions \ə di´shəns\ a form of articulatory defect in which sounds are added to words

additives \ad´i tivs\ chemicals added to food to enhance appearance, taste or preservative quality

adduction \ə duk´shən\ limb movement toward the midline

adenocarcinoma \ad´´e nō kär´´si nō´ mə\ type of malignant tumor derived from, or forming, glandular tissue

adenoids \ad´´ə noids´´\ lymphoid tissue located near the center of the posterior wall of the nasopharynx

adenoma \ad´´e nō´mə\ nonmalignant tumor of glandular origin

adenoma sebaceum \ad´´e nō mə se bā´sē əm\ tumorous nodules that often form a butterfly pattern on the faces of tuberous sclerosis patients

adiadochokinesia \ə dī´´ə dō´´kō ki nē´shə\ defective performance in making rapid alternating movements such as required in finger tapping; also spelled adiadokokinesia

adiaphoresis \ə dī´´ə fō rē´sis\ reduction or absence of perspiration

adipose \ad´i pōs\ fat or the condition of being fat

adiposogenital syndrome \ad´´i pos´ō jen i təl sin´ drōm\Fröhlich's syndrome

adipsia \ə dip´sē ə\ absence of thirst

adjunctive \ad junk´tiv\ providing assistance to a primary or central function

adjustment \ə just´mənt\ adaptation to changing conditions or environment

adolescence \ad´´ō le´sens\ temporal period in human growth and development that begins with the first signs of sexual maturation and ends when physical growth has been completed

adoption \ə dop´shən\ the legal taking of someone else's child for the purpose of raising him or her as one's own

adrenalin \ə dren´ə lin\ epinephrine

adult \ə dult´\ term designating the age of maturity and legal responsibility within a society

adultery \ə dul´tə rē\ socially disapproved extramarital sexual contact

adventitious \ad´´ven tish´əs\ accidental rather than hereditary

adventitiously deaf \ad´´ven tish´əs lē def\ inability to hear due to postnatal accident or disease

advocate \ad´vō kət\ one who presses for the rights of others

adynamia \ad´´i nā mē´ ə\ weakness or lack of strength

aerophagia \ăr´´ ō fä´jə\ habitual or compulsive swallowing of air

afebrile \ə fēb´rīl\ without fever

affect \af´fekt\ feelings or emotions

affectation \a´´fek tā´shən\ pretentious or unnatural behavior; mannerisms designed to create a special impression upon the observer

affection \ə fek´shən\ love, devotion,

fondness; a disease or abnormal condition

affective-volitional sphere \a fek´tiv-vō li´shən əl sfēr\ behavior that can be controlled by the mind or willpower; affective; pertaining to emotional state and volition; pertaining to power to choose

afferent \af´ėr ent\ referring to sensory impulses being transmitted from the peripheral to the central nervous system

affirmative action \ə fėr´mə tiv ak´shən\ a plan by which minority groups are assured greater participation in school enrollment or employment

affliction \ə flik´shən\ handicap or disorder

affricate \af´rə kit\ speech sound initiated by a plosive, as *ts* as in chew and *dz* as in jam

African Black \af´ri kən blak\ grade of marijuana grown in Africa

afterbirth \af´tėr bėrth\ material expelled from the uterus after the birth of a child, consisting mostly of placenta and amniotic membrane

after effect \af´tėr ē fekt\ delayed results of a disease, condition or medication

after image \af´´tėr im´əj\ visual image that persists subjectively after the cessation of stimulus

age \āj\ term of existence as measured by units of time; such terms as bone age, mental age, emotional age refer to developmental levels compared to group averages

age of onset \āj uv on´set\ the time in life that a particular disease or condition begins or becomes apparent

agenesis \ə jen´ə sis\ failure of an organ to develop

agent \ā´jent\ any factor or substance with capacity of acting upon an organism

ageusia \ə jū´shə\ defect in sense of taste

agglutinin \ə glü´ti nin\ an antibody in the blood serum causing particles (agglutinogens) to group in clumps

aggression \ə gresh´ən\ strong action (physical or verbal) directed by an individual against himself or herself, others or an inanimate object

agitated \aj´i tāt´´əd\ restless or hyperactive; performance marked by emotional distress, anxiety or fear

agitographia \ aj´´i tō gra´fē ə\ writing disability; writing with excessive rapidity, distortions and omissions

agitolalia \aj´´i tō lā´lē ə\ agitophasia

agitophasia \aj´´i tō fā´zhə\ excessively rapid speech with omissions, distortions and slurrings

aglaukopsia \ə glo kop´sē ə\ color blindness pertaining to shades of green

aglossia \ə glō´shə\ loss of the ability to speak; mutism; congenital absence of the tongue

aglutition \ag´´lü ti´shən\ difficulty in swallowing

aglycogeusia \ə glī´´kō jü´zhə\ inability to recognize sweetness

agnathia \ag nā´thē ə\ underdevelopment of the lower jaw

agnosia \ag nō´zhə\ defective ability to recognize or interpret familiar sensory stimulations

agonist \ag´ō nist\ major muscle responsible for a particular motion; agonist is opposed by the antagonist

agony \ag´ə nē\ extreme mental or physical pain; early symptoms of drug withdrawal

agoraphobia \ag´´ôr ə fō´bē ə\ chronic unreasonable fear of wide open spaces

agrammalogia \ə gram´ ə lō´jē ə\ inability to recall the correct structures of sentences; agrammatism; loss of ability to speak grammatically following brain damage; agramatologia

agrammatism \ə gram´ə tiz əm\ agrammalogia

agraphia \ə graf´ē ə\ defective writing ability due to central nervous system pathology

agromania \ag´´rō mā´nē ə\ abnormal desire to seek solitude with nature

agrypnia \ə grip´nē ə\ insomnia

aichmophobia \āk´´ mō fō´bē ə\ chronic, unreasonable fear of sharp objects

ailurophobia \ā lü´´rō fō´bē ə\ unreasonable fear of cats

airbone gap \ăr bŏn gap\ pure-tone hearing acuity difference between air conduction and bone conduction testing

air conduction \ăr kən duk´shən\ normal process of conducting sound waves through the ear canal to the drum membrane, as distinct from bone conduction

akinesia \ā´´ki nē´zhə\ defect in ability to move

akinesthesia \ə kin´´es thē´zhə\ defect of the movement sense which has to do with perceiving the changes that occur in joint angles

akinetic seizures \ā´´ki ne´tik sē´zhėrs\ sudden loss of postural balance usually accompanied by falling and a brief loss of consciousness

alalia \ə lā´lē ə\ decreased ability or inability to talk due to psychological or organic trauma

alaryngeal speech \ā´´lăr ən jē´əl spēch\ speech formed without benefit of a larynx

albedo \al bē´do\ percentage of light falling on a surface that is reflected by the surface; whiteness

Albers-Schönberg disease \al´bėrs-shōn´ bėrg di zēz\ a disorder in which there is abnormal thickening of bone; osteopetrosis or marble bone

albinism \al bī´niz əm\ lack of normal pigmentation of the eyes, hair and skin frequently attributed to an autosomal recessive hereditary trait

alcoholic \al´´kə hôl´ik\ compulsive drinker of alcoholic beverages

alcoholism \al´kə hôl´iz əm\ chronic excessive use of alcohol to the detriment of the user

alexia \ə lek´sē ə\ inability or decreased ability to read due to central nervous system pathology

algedonic \al´´jə don´ik\ describes feelings of pleasure or pain

algesia \al jē´zhə\ capacity to feel pain

algesthesia \al´´jəs thē´zhə\ sensitivity to sensory stimuli, as pain or touch

algolagnia \al´´gō lag´nē ə\ perversion based on sadism, masochism; sexual pleasure from inflicting or suffering pain

algophily \al gōf´i lē\ sexual deviation marked by desire to feel pain; algophilia

algophobia \al´´gō fō´bē ə\ chronic, unreasonable fear of pain

alienation \ā´´lē ə na´shən\ hostility, withdrawal or estrangement

alienist \āl´yə nist\ psychiatrist

alkalosis \al´´kə lō´sis\ increase of alkalinity in the body

alkapton bodies \al kap´tən bô´dēz\ group of substances possessing an affinity for alkali involved in causing alkaptonuria

alkaptonuria \al´´kap tə nėr´ē ə\ metabolic disorder characterized by urinary excretion of alkapton bodies; severe, prolonged cases may lead to arthritic symptoms

allele \ə lēl´\ either of two genes situated in the same genetic site that determine contrasting hereditary characterics, such as short/tall, straight/curly or light/dark

allergen \al´ėr jen\ any substance capable of eliciting an allergic response

allergic rhinitis \ə lėr´ jik rī nī´tis\ inflammation of the nose due to allergens

allergy \al´ėr jē\ hypersensitive state acquired through previous exposure to a particular substance (allergen) upon reexposure to the sensitizing substance (allergen); reactions such as skin rashes or sneezing

allesthesia \al´´es thē´zhə\ lack of sensitivity to touch

alloerotism \al´´ō ə rô´tiz əm\ sex drive directed toward another person, as opposed to autoerotism (toward oneself)

allolalia \al´´lō lā´lē ə\ speech defect

due to central nervous system pathology

allomorph \al´ə môrf´´\ a variation of sound that has the same meaning as a similar sound, for example, the final sounds of *slept* and *slipped* both indicate past tense

allophone \al´ō fōn\ sound subdivision of a phoneme

allosome \al´ə sōm\ sex chromosome; X or Y chromosome

alogia \ə lō´jə\ lack or loss of speech due to brain damage

aloofness \ə lüf´nes\ reserved manner; to maintain a social distance from others

alopecia \al´´ō pē´shə\ a disease in which the hair falls out; absence of hair from areas in which it normally grows

Alper's disease \al´pèrz di zēz´\ a syndrome due to gray matter degeneration; dementia is a feature, and patients are subject to seizures on a recurrent basis

alpha \al´fə\ first letter of the Greek alphabet; frequently used in scientific designations such as *alpha rays*

Alport's syndrome \al´pôrts sin´drōm\ a hereditary disease characterized by nephritis, deafness and ocular abnormalities

alter ego \äl´tèr ē´gō\ another self; a very close friend; a personal substitute

alveolar ridge \al´´vē ō´lèr rij\ upper or lower gum ridge containing the sockets that enclose the teeth

Alzheimer's disease \älts´ hī mèrs di zēz´\ early senile dementia

amalgam \ə mal´gəm\ mercury alloy

amathophobia \ə mə´´thō fō´bē ə\ unreasonable fear of dust and germs

amaurosis \am´´ə rō´sis\ loss of vision due to deterioration of the optic nerve

amaurotic family idiocy \am´´ə rôt´ik fam´i lē id´ē ə sē\ Tay-Sachs disease; an autosomal recessive lipid disorder

ambidexterity \am´´bi deks tăr´i tē\ equal skill of manipulation with either hand

ambient \am´bē ənt\ surrounding; circulating around

ambiguous \am big´ū əs\ having a variety of possible meanings

ambilateral \am´bi lat´èr əl\ both sides

ambiocular \am´´bē ôk´ū lèr\ using both eyes simultaneously and independently in the absence of convergence

ambiopia \am´´bē ōp´ē ə\ double vision; diplopia

ambisexual \am´´bē seks´ ū əl\ bisexual

ambivalence \am biv´ə lents\ simultaneous feelings of conflicting attitudes, such as love-hate

ambivert \am´bi vèrt\ an individual whose personality is intermediary between introversion and extroversion

amblyopia \am´´blē ō´pē ə\ visual defect without detectable eye pathology

amblyopia ex anopsia \am´´blē ō´pē ə eks an ōp´sē ə\ dimness of vision because of eye disease

ambosexual \am´´bō seks´ū əl\ affecting both sexes; bisexual; ambisexual

ambulatory \am´´bū lə tôr´ē\ able to walk; walking

amelia \ə mē´lē ə\ congenital absence of one or more limbs

amelioration \ə mēl´´yə rā´shən\ betterment; improvement; moderation of a condition

amenorrhea \ə men´´ō rē´ə\ absence of menstruation

ament \ā´ment\ one who was born mentally retarded

amentia \ə men´shə\ mental retardation

ameslan \am´əs lan\ American sign language

ametropia \am´´ə trō´pe ə\ structural defect of the eye that causes images to fail to focus properly on the retina

amimia \a mī´mē ə\ impairment in expressing one's self through gestures

amino acids \ə mē´nō a´sids\ basic components of proteins, many of which are essential for normal human growth and development

amnesia \am nē′zhə\ loss of memory

amniocentesis \am′′nē ō sen tē′sis\ medical procedure whereby amniotic fluid is removed from the uterus for study or diagnostic purposes

amnion \am′nē ôn\ membrane that contains the fetus

amniotic fluid \am′′nē ô′tik flü′id\ fluid within the amnion that surrounds the fetus

amniotic sac \am′′nē ô′tik sak\ thin membrane that encloses the fetus; amnion

amoral \ā môr′əl\ lacking moral judgment or sensibility; not concerned with moral standards

amorphous \ə môr′fus\ not having a definite or predictable shape

amorphus \amôr′fus\ shapeless defective fetus

amphetamine \am fet′ə min\ central nervous stimulant or drug frequently used as an appetite depressant; also used illegally within the drug culture

amphiarthrosis \am′′fē är thrō′sis\ condition in which there is reduced motion in a joint due to fibrocartilage between the two surfaces

amplifier \ am′′pli fī′ér\ electrical device to increase the volume of sound

amputation \am′′pū tā′shən\ removal of all or portions of a limb or appendage

amputee \am′′pū tē\ individual with one or more limbs wholly or partially removed

amusia \ə mū′zhə\ inability to produce or understand musical sounds

amyotonia \ə mī′′ō tō′nē ə\ decreased muscle tone; weakness of all muscles of the body

amyotonia congenita \ə mī′′ō tō′nē ə kôn jen′i tə\ congenital defect characterized by muscular hypotonia; Oppenheim's disease

anabolism \ə nab′ə liz əm\ normal metabolic process, changing food to living tissue; building up of the body substance

anaclisis \ə nak′lə sis\ dependence upon others for emotional support

anaclitic choice \an′′ə klit′ik chois\ the selection of a mate who resembles a person one depended upon during infancy or childhood

anaclitic depression \an′′ə klit′ik dē presh′ən\ a depression seen in infants who have been separated from their mothers in their early months that may result in inability to achieve normal interpersonal relationships later in life

anaerobe \an′′ə rōb\ microorganism that lives in oxygen free environments, such as anaerobic bacteria

anakusis \an′′ ə kü′sis\ total deafness; anacusia; anacusis

anal \ān′əl\ pertaining to the anus; in psychoanalytic terms, refers to a personality type characterized by excessive cleanliness and orderliness

anal character \ān′əl kăr′ək tér\ a personality that manifests so-called anal traits: cleanliness, orderliness and stubbornness

anal phase \ān′əl fāz\ term describing a child from eight months to about the fourth year

analgesia \an′′əl jē′zhə\ reduced sensitivity or insensitivity to pain

analgesic \an′′əl jē′zik\ pain-relieving substance

analysand \ə nal′ə sand\ client receiving psychoanalytic treatment

analysis \ə nal′i sis\ process of separating a substance or problem into understandable component parts

analyst \an′ə list\ accredited therapist who performs psychoanalytic services; practitioner of psychoanalysis

anamnesis \an′′əm nē′sis\ memory; personal or case history of a patient

ananabasia \an an′ə bā′zhə\ inability to climb stairs or heights

anaphase \an′ə fāz\ stage in mitosis when the divided chromosomes move toward the spindle poles

anaphoresis \an′′ə fō rē′sis\ insufficient activity or malfunctioning of the sweat glands

anaphrodisia \an´´af rō di´zhə\ diminished sex drive

anaphylaxis \an´´ə fē lak´sis\ pronounced allergic reaction to foreign substances, as with bee stings or drugs

anaplasty \an´ə plas´´tē\ plastic surgery

anarthria \an aï´ thrē ə\ inability to articulate speech or writing due to brain lesion or damage to peripheral nerves that innervate the articulatory muscles

anathema \ə nath´ə mə\ a curse; a hated person or thing

anatomical age \an´´ə tom´i kəl āj\ the apparent age of the body or its parts as compared to the chronological age

ancillary \an´sil lăr´´e\ refers to assistance in performance of a duty, service or program

ancillary services \an´sil lăr e sėr´vis əs\ functional units that support a major program; in certain circumstances, for example, speech therapy, psychotherapy or physical therapy might be considered ancillary services to total medical rehabilitation

androgen \an´drə jən\ male sex hormone

androgynous \an droj´ə nəs\ having both male and female physical characteristics; hermaphroditic

anecdotal record \an´´ek dŏt´əl rek´ərd\ written summary of behavior used to assist in understanding a subject's functioning

anechoic chamber \an´´ə kō´ik chăm´bėr\ a soundproof room used for measuring hearing acuity

anemia \ə nē´mē ə\ deficiency of hemoglobin or red blood cells that leads to weakness and lack of vigor in an individual

anencephalus \an´´en sef´ə ləs\ a fetus suffering from anencephaly

anencephaly \an´´en sef´ə lē\ defective condition wherein part or all of the brain may be missing

anesthesia \an´´es thē´zhə\ inability to feel or perceive sensations, especially inability to feel pain

aneuploidy \an´´ü ploi´dē\ a state of having more or less than the normal diploid chromosome count

aneurysm \an´ū riz´´əm\ weakness in the walls of a vein or artery that may expand and put pressure on surrounding tissue or rupture resulting in death or central nervous system damage; aneurism

anginal attacks \an jī´nəl ə taks´\ steady severe pain and feeling of pressure in region of the heart

angiocardiography \an´´jē ō kär´´ dē ôg´rə fē\ a radiographic examination of the heart and circulatory system

angioma \an´jē o´mə\ tumor that forms in lymph or blood vessels

angular gyrus \ang´gyə lėr jī´rəs\ part of the brain that controls certain speech functions

anhedonia \an´´ hē dō´nē ə\ inability to enjoy the pleasures of life

anhidrosis \an´´hi drō´sis\ diminished or complete absence of secretion of sweat

aniridia \an´´i rid´ē ə\ congenital absence of the iris of the eye

aniseidominance \an´´i sī dôm´i nənts\ visual defect in which a person sees images brighter in one eye than the other

aniseikonia \an´´i sī kō´nē ə\ visual defect in which images differ in size or shape between the two eyes

anisocoria \an´´i sō côr´e ə\ differing pupil size between the two eyes

anisometropia \an´i sō mə trō´pē ə\ difference of the refractive power of the two eyes

ankylosing spondylitis \ang´ki lō´sing spon´´di lī´tis\ a crippling condition characterized by back stiffness, caused by involvement of the sacroiliac and other joints; one of the arthritidies

ankylosis \ang´ki lō sis\ consolidation of a joint

anoia \ə noi´yə\ mental retardation

anomaly \ə nom´ə lē\ deviation from the normal condition

anomia \ə nō´mē ə\ inability to associate

persons, places or things with their names

anomie \an´ə mē\ absence of norms, especially norms of social conduct; anomy

anophthalmia \an´´of thal´mē ə\ congenital absence of the eyes

anophthalmos \an´´ of thal´ mōs\ absence of the eyeball; anophthalmia

anopia \an ō´pē ə\ absence or hypoplasia of an eye

anopsia \an op̄´sē ə\ condition in which the vision of an eye is suppressed as in heterotropia

anorchism \an ôr´kiz əm\ congenital absence of one or both testicles

anorexia \an´´ō rek´sē ə\ loss of appetite or inability to eat

anorexia nervosa \an´´ō rek´sē ə nèr vō´sə\ emotional disorder in which an individual rejects food to the point of starvation, emaciation and even death

anorgasmy \an ôr gaz´mē\ inability to reach sexual climax or orgasm

anorthopia \an´´ôr thə pē ə\ condition characterized by distorted vision

anosmia \an ōz´mē ə\ impairment in sense of smell

anoxemia \an´´ok sē´mē ə\ serious state of oxygen reduction in the blood

anoxia \an´´ok sē´ə\ lack of oxygen

antagonist \an tag´ō nist\ muscle that acts in opposition to a major muscle in an action; opposite or against

antecedent event \an´´tə sē´dənt ē vent\ occurrence that precedes a response that is judged to have an association with the response

ante partum \an´tē pär´təm\ temporal reference to period before childbirth

anterior \an tēr´ē ėr\ before; in front of; front part

anterior chamber \an tēr´ē ėr chām´bér\ aqueous space in front of eye between cornea and iris

anteversion \an´´tə vėr zhən\ a bending or tipping forward of a bone, organ or body part

anthropometry \an´´thrō pom´ə trē\ science that is concerned with measurements of the human body

antibiotic \an´´tī bī ôt´ik\ antagonistic to life; group of drugs used to destroy bacteria within a living organism

antibody \an´tī bôd´´ē\ protein substance produced in an animal to combat the toxic effects of antigens

anticonvulsant \an´´ti kon vul´sənt\ medication that acts to control seizures

antidote \an´ti dōt\ substance or procedure used to counteract or ameliorate the effects of a poison or stressful situation

antiepileptic \an´´tē ep´e lep´´tik\ preventing or reducing epileptic seizure activity

antigen \an´ti jen\ substances produced by an animal that stimulate the production of antibodies

antihemorrhagic \an´´tē hēm ō raj´ik\ preventative or controlling of hemorrhage or bleeding

antihypnotic drug \an´´ti hip nôt´ik drug\ drug that hinders sleep

antimetropia \an´´ti mə trō´pē ə\ condition in which one eye is hyperopic while the other eye is myopic

antiphlogistic \an´´tē flō jis´tik\ control or relief of an inflammation

antipruritic \an´´tē prü ri´tik\ medication to relieve itching

antipyretic \an´´tē pī ret´ ik\ medication to reduce fever

antiseptic \an´´ti sep´tik\ substance that inhibits the growth of microorganisms

antisocial \an´´tē sō´shəl\ self-centered; hostile or apathetic to other people

antisocial behavior \an´´ti sō´shəl bē hāv´yėr\ conduct contrary to accepted social mores

antispasmodic \an´´tē spaz môd´ik\ relieving or preventing spasms

antitoxin \an´´ti tok´sən\ antibody to the poison produced by a microorganism

anxiety \ang zī´i tē\ emotional state characterized by fear, worry, uneasiness and apprehension

aorta \ā ôr´ tə\ the main artery emerging from the left ventricle of the heart that distributes blood flow to all parts of the body

aortic stenosis \ā ȯr´tik stə nō´ sis\ a defect of the aorta in which there is a narrowing of its diameter at its orifice

apareunia \ap´´ə rü´nē ə\ inability to have sexual intercourse

apathetic \ap´´ə thet´ik\ not demonstrating feelings; lacking vigor

apathy \ap´ə thē\ uncaring, indifferent, or lacking vigor

apastia \ə pās´te ə\ refusal to eat due to neurological involvement

apepsia \ə pep´sē ə\ indigestion

Apert's syndrome \ā´pėrts sin´drōm\ acrocephalosyndactyly

aphagia \ə fā´jē ə\ refusal to eat; aversion to food

aphakia \ə fā´kē ə\ congenital absence of the lens in the eye

aphalangia \a´´fə lan´jē ə\ absence of phalanges of hands or feet

aphasia \ə fā´zhə\ disability in communication that may be manifested in varying degrees of defect in comprehension or expression of speech, writing or sign language due to central nervous system pathology

aphemia \ə fē´mē ə\ inability to vocalize or to speak intelligently

aphephobia \af´´ə fō´bē ə\ chronic fear of touching or of being touched

aphonia \ə fō´nē ə\ loss of voice

aphrasia \ə frā´zhə\ inability to speak or write intelligently due to paralysis or deliberate avoidance

aphrodisia \af´´rō dē´zhə\ sexual stimulation; abnormal or extreme sexual excitement

aphrodisiac \af´´rō dē´zē ak\ agent that stimulates sexual desire

aphrodisiomania \af´´rō diz´ē ō mā´nē ə\ preoccupation with sex

aphronesia \af´´rō nē´zhə\ mental illness; dementia

aphthenxia \af thenk´sē ə\ impairment of articulation

aplasia \ə plā´zhə\ underdevelopment or lack of development of an organ or body part

apnea \ap´nē ə\ temporary stoppage of respiration

apodia \ə pō´dē ə\ congenital absence of one or both feet

aponia \ə pō´nē ə\ absence of pain

apoplexy \ap´ ə plek´sē\ a stroke resulting in coma and paralysis

apostasy \ə pos´tə sē\ a sudden and complete abandonment of one's position, principles, religion, cause, etc.

apparatus \ap´´ə rat´əs\ coordinated group of instruments, machines, or structures designed to perform a specific function

apperception \ap´´ėr sep´shən\ ability to receive, interpret and understand sensory stimulations

appersonation \a ṗer´´sə nā´shən\ the unconscious appropriation of the personality and characteristics of another (usually well-known) person

appetence \ap´ə tens\ strong desire or craving

appraisal \ə prā´zəl\ evaluation; estimation of quality or worth

apprehension \ap´´rə hen´shən\ feeling of fear, dread or foreboding

apraxia \ə prak´sē ə\ impairment in ability to make purposeful movements

aprosexia \ap´´rə sek´se ə\ inability to maintain attention, to concentrate, especially due to defective hearing, sight or mental weakness

apselaphesia \ap´´sēl ə fē´zhə\ insensitivity to touch or absence of tactile sense

aptitude \ap´ti tüd\ natural ability before training or practice

aptitude test \ap´ti tüd test\ a test that can predict possible success in performance or reaction

apyrexia \ə pī rek´sē ə\ absence of fever

aquaphobia \äk´´wə fō´bē ə\ morbid fear of water

aqueous humor \ä´kwē əs hū´mėr\ fluid that fills the eye

arachnodactyly \ə rak´´nō dak´ti lē\ Marfan's syndrome

ardanesthesia \ar´´dan es thē´zhə\ insensitivity or inability to feel heat

Argyll Robertson pupil \är´gīl rob´ėrt

sən pū´pil\ pupil that responds normally to accommodation but responds poorly to light

aristogenesis \ə ris´´tō jen´ə sis\ the gradual improvement of genetic mechanisms through adaptation

aristogenics \ə ris´´tō jen´iks\ the improvement of a race through selective, optimal breeding

arithmomania \ə rith´´mō mā´nē ə\ excessive preoccupation with counting things; abnormal concern with numbers and numerical functions

Arnold-Chiari syndrome \är´nəld-kē är´ē sin´drōm\ cerebral defect characterized by herniation of brain tissue into the spinal canal

arrested hydrocephalus \ə res´təd hī´´drō sef´ə ləs\ status when the unnatural accumulation of cerebrospinal fluid ceases due to either surgical intervention or a natural process

arrhythmia \ə rith´mē ə\ lack of normal or usual rhythm

arteriosclerosis \är tēr´´ ē ō sklə rō´sis\ hardening of the artery walls

arthritis \är thrī´tis\ inflammation of a joint

arthrodesis \är´thrə dē´sis\ the fixation of a joint through surgical procedures

arthrogryposis \är´´thrō grī pō´sis\ a crippling disease in which the joints are stiff and unbending

arthroplasty \är´´thrō plas´tē\ surgical restructuring of joints

articulation \är tik´´ū lā´shən\ in anatomy, articulation refers to the connection of two or more bones of the skeletal system; in speech therapy, articulation refers to the enunciation of words and phrases

articulators \är´´tik ū lā´tərs\ body parts involved in speech production

articulatory defect \är´´tik ū´lə tôr´ē dē´fekt\ indistinct speech due to faulty vocalization of speech sounds

artificial larynx \är´´ti fi´shəl lăr´inks\ electronic device to provide sound for vocal function

art therapy \art thăr´ ə pē\ the use of art

as a tool for releasing emotional tension and as nonverbal communication

arytenoid cartilage \är´´ə tē´noid kär´ti ləj\ the jug-shaped cartilage of the larynx

asapholalia \as´´ə fō lā´lē ə\ speech characterized by mumblings

asemasia \ās´´ ə mā´zhə\ loss or diminished communicative ability; asemia

asemia \ə sē´mē a\ inability to understand speech, writing or other communication symbols

aseptic \ə sep´tik\ free from bacteria or fungi

asexual \ā sek´shū əl\ lacking sex or functional sexual organs

asitia \ə si´shə\ loathing stimulated at the thought or sight of food

asonia \ə sō´nē ə\ tone deafness; less than normal ability to distinguish between different frequencies of sound

aspecific \ā´´spə sif´ik\ not due to a particular cause or origin

asphyxia \as fik´sē ə\ suffocation; condition brought on by lack of air

asphyxia neonatorum \as fik´sē ə nē´´ō nā tôr´um\ oxygen deprivation of the newborn

aspirate \as´pi rāt\ to breathe or draw air or other substances into the lungs

aspiration \as´´pi rā´shən\ expulsion of air during speech; goal level for a particular endeavor

assertiveness \ə sėr´tiv nəs\ the ability to express one's needs, rights and opinions

assessment \ə ses´mənt\ evaluation

assimilation \ə sim´i lā´shən\ the integration of ideas, concepts, knowledge into a person's belief structure, the metabolizing of food

association \ə sōs´´ē ā´shən\ mental connections between sensations, memories and ideas

associative learning \ə sō´shə tiv lėr´ning\ rate of learning and memory; theory that ideas and objects are linked

astasia-abasia \ə stā´zhə-ə bā´zhə\ functional impairment in the ability to walk in the absence of detectable organic pathology even though the legs may otherwise be moved normally

astereognosis \ə stēr''ē ôg nō'sis\ impairment in ability to identify objects through the sense of touch

asthenia \as thē'nē ə\ weakness; listlessness; lack of enthusiasm and drive

asthenopia \as''thə nō'pē ə\ eye fatigue resulting in pain and dimness of vision

asthma \az'mə\ respiratory disease marked by coughing and wheezing; some cases may be due to allergenic reactions; emotional stress may be a factor

astigmatism \ə stig'mə tiz''əm\ visual defect caused by irregular curvature of the lens of the eye that results in blurred or indistinct vision on certain visual planes

astraphobia \as''trə fō'bē ə\ chronic, unreasonable fear of storms, especially thunder and lightning

asylum \ə sī'ləm\ an institution for the care of the retarded, mentally ill or other types of severely handicapped persons

asymbolia \as''im bō'lē ə\ inability to understand words, gestures or other symbols

asymmetry \ə sim'ə trē\ decreased similarity of corresponding parts on opposite sides of the body

asymptomatic \ā simp''tə ma'tik\ without symptoms or signs of a disease or condition

asynergia \ā''sin ėr'jē ə\ lack of muscular coordination

ataraxia \at''ə rak'sē ə\ a tranquil state; freedom from anxiety and worry

atavism \at'ə viz''əm\ inheritance from a distant ancestor; sometimes referred to as a reversion or throwback

ataxia \ə tak'sē ə\ defect in balance and coordination due to central nervous system pathology

ataxiaphasia \ə tak''sē ə fā'zhə\ condition in which there is a defect in structuring sentences properly

ataxia-telangiectasia \ə tak'sē ə-tel''an jek tā'zhə\ hereditary, progressive condition characterized by visual defects, multiple angiomas and respiratory infections

ataxophemia \ə tak''sō fē'mē ə\ incoordination of speech muscles

ataxophobia \ə tak''sō fō'bē ə\ chronic, morbid fear of disorder

atelectasis \at''ə lek'tə sis\ lack of lung expansion at birth; postnatal lung collapse

athetoid \ath'ə toid\ affected with athetosis

athetosis \ath''ə tō'sis\ form of cerebral palsy in which the patient is subject to involuntary, uncontrollable movement of the body, face and extremities resulting in strange movement patterns; these motions are present to some extent whenever the subject is awake and may increase when voluntary movement is attempted

athrepsia \ə threp'sē ə\ severe starvation in an infant; marasmus

athreptic \ə threp'tik\ relating to or suffering from progressive wasting and emaciation

atonia \ā tō'nē ə\ decreased muscle tone

atonic \ə tōn'ik\ relaxed; without tension or tone

atonicity \ā''tō ni'si tē\ inability of muscles to contract

atresia \ə trē'zhə\ congenital closure of a body opening or passageway that is normally supposed to be open

atrophy \a'trə fē\ shrinking in size of an organ, muscle or body part

attachment \ə tach'mənt\ fixation; affectionate regard

attack \ə tak\ a sudden onslaught by a symptom, seizure, condition or disease

attendant \ə ten'dənt\ nonprofessional child care workers in an institution or hospital

attention span \ə ten'shən span\ limit of time a person can maintain concentration on a particular task or activity

attenuation \ə ten''ū ā'shən\ reduction

in intensity, as in pain or fever; to reduce in strength

attitude \at´ə tüd\ preferential belief or feeling established by experience

attitude scale \at´ə tüd skāl\ device to measure strength of attitudes or feelings

atypical \ā tip´i kəl\ different from the average or ordinary

audible \ä´di bəl\ capable of being detected by hearing

audile \ä´dēl\ that faculty of recalling auditory memories

auding \ä´ding\ listening, recognizing and understanding spoken words

audiogenic \ä´´dē ō jen´ik\ caused or produced by sound as in audiogenic epileptic attacks

audiogram \ä´dē ō gram´´\ chart recording hearing acuity at different frequencies of sound

audiologist \ä´´dē ôl´ə jist\ hearing specialist

audiology \ä´´dē ôl´ō jē\ study of the entire field of hearing including the anatomy and function of the ear, impairment of hearing and the education or reeducation of persons with hearing loss

audiometer \ä´´dē ôm´ə tér\ electronic device used to test hearing acuity at various sound frequencies and intensities

audiometric zero \ä´´dē ō me´trik zēr´ō\ zero decibles as measured by an audiometer

audiometry \ä´´dē ôm´ ə trē\ testing of the hearing sense

audiovisual \ä´´dē ō viz´ū əl\ stimulation of both the senses of hearing and vision

audition \ä´di shən\ the hearing sense; the process of being heard

auditory \ä´di tôr´´ē\ referring to the sense of hearing

auditory acuity \ä´di tôr´´ē ə kū´i tē\ sharpness of hearing ability

auditory agnosia \ä´di tôr´´ē ag nō´zhə\ inability to recognize or interpret sounds

auditory aphasia \ä´d tôr´´ē ə fā´shə\ defect, loss or nondevelopment of the ability to comprehend spoken words due to disease, injury or maldevelopment of the hearing centers of the brain; word deafness; same as receptive aphasia

auditory decoding \ä´di tôr´´ē dē kōd´ing\ ability to understand spoken language

auditory discrimination \ä´di tôr´´e dis krim´´ə nā´shən\ ability to discriminate between sounds of different frequency, intensity and pressure pattern components; ability to distinguish one speech sound from another

auditory memory \ä´di tôr´´ē mem´ə rē\ ability to recall sounds previously heard

auditory memory span \ä´di tôr´´ē mem´ə rē span\ related or unrelated items that can be recalled immediately after hearing them

auditory nerve \a´di tôr´´ē nérv\ the eighth cranial nerve, which transmits sound from the inner ear to the brain

auditory perception \ä´di tôr´´ē pér sep´shən\ mental awareness of sound

auditory sequencing \ä´di tôr´´ē sē´kwen sing\ ability to recall information previously heard in correct order and sequence

auditory training \ä´di tôr´´ē trān´ing\ training and therapy that aids a hearing impaired person in better utilizing residual hearing

auditory-visual integration \ä´di tôr´´ē-viz´ū əl in´´tə grā´shən\ the association of what is seen and heard with its printed name or symbol

aura \är´ə\ sensation preceding and forewarning an epileptic seizure

aural \är´əl\ pertaining to the ear or hearing

auricle \är´i kəl\ portion of the external ear not contained within the head

autism \ä´tiz əm\ withdrawal or absorption in fantasy, including personal and social isolation

autochthonous \ä tôk´thə nəs\ originating within the organism with outside stimulation

autocriticism \ä´´tō kri´ti siz´´əm\ self-evaluation of one's behavior, personality, thought processes or philosophy

autoeroticism \ä´´tō ē rot´i siz əm\ masturbation, solitary self-gratification of sexual desires; autoerotism

autogenous \ä tôj ə nəs\ originating within; endogenous

autokinesis \ä´´tō ki nē´sis\ movement stimulated from within the organism

automatism \ä tom´ə tiz əm\ performance of nonhabitual acts without conscious intent

autonomic \ä´´tō nom´ik\ without external control

autonomic nervous system \ä´´tō nom´ik nėr´vəs sis´təm\ nerve system that regulates the smooth muscles and glands

autonomic seizures \ä´´tō nom´ik sē´zhėrs\ sudden hypotensive states, including salivation, flushing and excessive intestinal activity

autophilia \ä´´tō fil´ē ə\ narcissism; excessive love of one's self

autophobia \ä´´tō fō´ bē ə\ a chronic, unremitting fear of being alone

autoplasty \ä´´tō plas´tē\ the repair of a body part using tissue from another part of the body

autoscopy \ä tōs´kə pē\ visual hallucination in which the person sees his own image

autosomal dominant gene \ä´´tō sōm´ əl dom´i nənt jēn\ refers to a gene located in the autosomes that pro-

duces its effect in the presence of a contrasting gene

autosomal recessive gene \ä´´tō sōm´əl rē ses´iv jēn\ refers to a gene located in the autosomes that fails to produce its effect in the presence of a contrasting gene

autosome \ä´tō sōm\ all paired chromosomes except the sex chromosomes

autosuggestion \ä´´tō sug jes´chən\ suggestion originating within one's self; internal repetition of a thought in order to strengthen one's outlook, determinination, health, etc.

autotelic \ä´´tō tēl´ik\ referring to basic functioning and survival traits

autotopagnosia \ä´´tō top´´əg nō´zhə\ inability to orient one's self to one's own body parts correctly

aversion therapy \ə vėr´zhən thăr´ə pē\ the use of punishment to socialize autistic children

aversive stimulus \ə vėr´siv stim´ū ləs\ a consequence that would tend to reduce the behavior that it follows

axiology \ak´´sē ôl´ə jē\ the study of value systems; the practice of applying moral values to date

axon \aks´on\ the part of a nerve cell that conducts the nerve impulses away from the cell body

azoospermia \ā´´zü spėr´ mē ə\ lack of sperm in the semen

Aztec idiocy \az´tek id´ē ə sē\ microcephaly

B **babbling** \bab´ling\ meaningless speech; seemingly random production of different speech sounds

babelism \bab´ə liz´´əm\ confusion of thought processes and speech

Babinski reflex \bə bin´skē rē´fleks\ a muscular reaction in which the big toe extends when the sole of the foot is scratched; the reflex is normal in infants but considered a sign of neurological defect when present in adults

baby talk \bā´bē täk\ the vocalization by older individuals of speech sounds commonly used by children in early stages of speech and language development

bacillophobia \bə sil´´ō fō´bē ə\ chronic, unreasonable fear of disease-causing microorganisms

backward chaining \bak´werd chān´ing\ a teaching process in which a task is broken down into successive steps to the terminal behavior, and the steps are mastered in reverse order of their usual sequence

backward child \bak´werd chīld\ outmoded term for mentally retarded child

bacteremia \bak´tə rē´mē ə\ blood poisoning

ballism \bäl´iz əm\ ballismus

ballismus \bə liz´mus\ form of motor dysfunction characterized by jerking, twitching and swinging movements of limbs

ballistograph \bə lis´tō graf\ a device for measuring the hyperactivity of children

balneology \bal´´nē ol´ə jē\ the science of therapeutic use of bathing

balneotherapy \bal´´nē ō thăr´ə pē\ treatment of disorders by bathing

barbiturate \bär bit´ū rāt\ group of drugs used as central nervous depressants

barbiturism \bär bich´ə riz´´im\ chronic poisoning due to use of barbituric acid derivative

baresthesia \bär´´es thē´zhə\ sensitivity to pressure or weight

barognosis \bar´´əg nō´sis\ the ability to perceive weight differences

barotitis \bär´ə tī´tis\ inflammation of the ears due to sudden changes in atmospheric pressure; baro-otitis

barotrauma \bär´ə trä´mə\ damage to the ear caused by sudden change in atmospheric pressure

Barr body \bär bo´dē\ sex chromatin representing the inactive or resting chromosome

barren \băr´ən\ sterile; incapable of producing offspring

baryecoia \bär´i koi´yə\ impaired hearing

baryencephalia \bär´i en sə fā´lē ə\ mental retardation

barylalia \bär´i läl´yə\ thick, indistinct, husky speech; baryphonia

baryphonia \bär´´i fō´nē ə\ a thick, husky quality of voice

barythymia \bär´´i thī´mē ə\ deep mental depression; melancholia

basal age \bā´səl aj\ highest mental age score secured on a psychological test

basal metabolism rate \bā´səl mə tab´ ə liz əm rāt\ amount of energy expended to maintain vital life processes

baseline \bās´līn\ level of behavioral functioning of an individual prior to treatment or intervention

basophobia \bā´´sə fō´bē ə\ unreasonable fear of losing ability to walk; fear of walking

basic anxiety \bā´sik ang zī´i tē\ troubled feeling of helplessness in a potentially hostile world

bastard \bas´tėrd\ one born out of wedlock; illegitimate

bathmophobia \bath´´mō fō´be ə\ bathophobia

bathophobia \bath´´ō fō´be ə\ morbid fear of looking down from high places; bathmophobia

battarism \bat´ə riz əm\ stammering or stuttering

Batten, Spielmeyer-Vogt, Kufs' disease \ bat´ən, spēl´muer-vōt, kūfs di zēz´\ juvenile, amaurotic familial idiocy

battered child syndrome \bat´ėrd

20

chīld sin´drōm\ condition in which children are physically abused by their parents or other adults

battology \bə tol´a jē\ excessive, boring repetition of words in speaking or writing

Beard's syndrome \bērds sin´drōm\ neurasthenia; weakness and exhaustion following depression

bedlam \bed´ləm\ state of uproar and confusion; slang for hospital for the mentally ill

bedwetting \bed´wet ing\ enuresis; involuntary urination during sleep

behavior \bē hāv´yėr\ act, response or movement of an animal

behavioral analysis \bē hāv yėr əl ə nal´ə sis\ method used to systematically identify changes in a person's functioning as a result of educational or psychological programming

behavioral model \bē hāv´yėr əl mod´əl\ theory based on assumption that behavior disorders are primarily the result of poor or inappropriate learning

behavioral rigidity \bē hāv´ yėr əl ri jid´i te\ inability to cope with new situations

behavioral sciences \bē hāv´yėr əl sī´ən səs\ study of human action and behavior with the aim of establishing generalizations regarding such behavior

behaviorism \bē hāv´yėr iz´´əm\ division of psychology that is mainly concerned with overt, measurable, definable behavior of animals

behavorist \bē hav´yėr ist\ one who follows the doctrines of behaviorism

behavior modification \bē hāv´yėr mod´´i fi kā´shən\ systematic management of individual with the intent of altering observable behaviors

Bell's palsy \belz päl´zē\ paralysis on one side of the face due to facial nerve involvement

belonephobia \bel´´o nə fō´bē ə\ morbid fear of sharp objects

benefactor \ben´ə fak´´tėr\ guardian or foster parent for a handicapped person

benign \bē nīn´\ not malignant; doing little or no harm

benign tumor \bē nīn´ tü´mer\ growth that is not malignant, not invading surrounding territory

beriberi \băr´ē băr´ē\ neuromuscular disease associated with malnutrition and vitamin B_1 (thiamine) deficiency

berserk \bėr sėrk´\ in a violent rage

bestiality \bēs´´tē al´ i tē\ sexual interaction of a person with an animal

bibliophobia \bib´´lē ō fō´bē ə\ abnormal fear or dislike of books

bicultural \bī´kul chėr´´əl\blending and integration of two different cultures

bifocal lenses \bī fō´kəl lenz´əs\ two lenses in glasses with the upper lens assisting in distance vision, the lower lens correcting near vision

bilabial \bī lā´bē əl\ consonant sound, like *p*, *b* or *m*, formed with both lips

bilateral \bī lat´ėr əl\ pertaining to or involving both sides

bile \bīl\ liver secretion that helps break up and digest fats

bilingual \bī ling´gwəl\ possessing facility in two languages

bilirubin \bil´´ē rü´bən\ red bile pigment that is found free in the bloodstream as a result of red blood cell destruction in certain hemolytic diseases such as Rh factor incompatibility

bilirubin encephalopathy \bil´´ē rü´bən en sef´´ə lôp´ə thē\ central nervous system pathology as a result of bilirubinemia

bimanual \bī man´ū əl\ the requirement or ability to use both hands adequately

bimodal \bi mōd´əl\ having two peaks or concentrations in a statistical distribution curve

binaural \bīn ôr´əl\ pertaining to both ears

binocular \bə nok´yə lėr\ pertaining to both eyes

binocular vision \bə nok´yə lėr vi´zhən\ ability to focus both eyes on a single object so as to perceive a single image

binotic \bī not´ik\ pertaining to both ears

biochemistry \bī´´ō kem´i strē\ study of chemical processes within living organisms

biofeedback \bī´´o fēd´bak\ technique in which electronic instruments are used to amplify and control changes in the body, such as heart rate, blood pressure, skin temperature, muscle relaxation and the production of certain brain waves

biogenesis \bī´´ō jen´ə sis\ the origin of life

biogenetics \ bī´´o jə ne´ tiks\ study of the origin of organisms

biological model \bī´´ō loj´i kəl mod´əl\ theory based on assumption that behavior disorders are primarily the result of central nervous system malfunction

biometry \bi om´ə trē\ application of statistical procedures to evaluate biological data

biopsy \bī´op sē\ examination of tissue removed from a living subject

biosocial \bī´´ō sō´shəl\ the interaction of biological and social factors

biotic \bī ôt´ik\ pertaining to living substance

biparous \bip´ə rəs\ refers to the birth of twins

biracial \bī´rā shəl\ composed of two different races

birth control \bėrth kən trōl´\ the regulation of the number of children born by limiting conception

birth injury \bėrth in´jə rē\ injury sustained during the birth process

birth trauma \bėrth trä´mə\ trauma during the birth process

bisexual \bī sek´shü əl\ having physical characteristics of both sexes; a hermaphrodite

blastophthoria \blas´´tof thō´rē ə\ gene damage causing mental retardation

bleeder \blēd´ėr\ hemophiliac

blepharitis \blef´´ə rī´tis\ inflammation of the eyelid

blepharoplegia \blef´´ə rō plē´jē ə\ paralysis of the eyelid

blepharoptosis \blef´´ə rō tō´sis\ drooping eyelid due to paralysis

blepharospasm \blef´´ə rō spaz´əm\ uncontrolled winking due to spasms, eyestrain or anxiety

blind \blīnd\ unable to see; those who have no sight or whose sight is so defective that they required education by methods not involving the use of sight

blindism \blīnd´iz əm\ mannerism often found among the blind, such as head rolling and rocking

blindness \blīnd´nəs\ inability or severely diminished ability to see; in the U. S., a visual defect of 20/200 or less in the better eye after correction usually constitutes legal blindness

blind spot \blīnd spot\ light insensitive point where the optic nerve enters the retina

Bliss method \blis meth´əd\ a nonverbal communication system used with the severely handicapped

blocking \blok´ing\ difficulties in recalling repressed or anxiety-producing thoughts

blue baby \blü bā´bē\ infant born with cyanosis

boarding home \bôr´ding hōm\ community residential facility for the handicapped

Bobath method \bō´bath meth´əd\ system of neuromuscular rehabilitation used with the cerebral palsied

body image \bo´dē im´əj\ knowledge of and regard for one's own body

bone age \bōn āj\ predicting growth in terms of bone development

bone conduction \bōn con duk´shən\ transmission of sound waves through the head bones to the inner ear (as distinguished from air conduction)

borderline retardates \bôr´dėr līn rē tär´dāts\ classification of individuals with I.Q. range between 70 and 80

botulism \bôt´chə liz´əm \ poisoning that results from improperly preserved or canned food due to the toxin of an anaerobic organism

Bourneville's disease \bėr´nə vils di zēz´´\ tuberous sclerosis; epiloia

brace \brās\ orthotic device used to support a body part, to relieve weakness or to maintain alignment

brachial \brā´kē əl\ pertaining to the arm

brachial birth palsy \brā´kē əl bėrth päl´zē\ paralysis or partial paralysis of an arm due to injury of the nerves of the brachial plexus at birth

Brachmann-de Lange syndrome \bräk´man dē länj sin´drōm\ another name for Cornelia de Lange's syndrome

brachycephaly \brak´´ə sef´ə lē\ head that is flattened posteriorly

brachygnathia \brak´´ə nā´thē ə\ small lower jaw

brachyphalangia \brak´´ē fə lan´jē ə\ abnormal shortness of the bones of the fingers and toes (phalanges)

bradyacusia \brā´´dē ə kü´zhə\ reduced hearing acuity

bradyarthia \brā´´dē är´thē ə\ slow and labored speech

bradycardia \brā´´dē cär´dē ə\ slow heartbeat or heart action

bradyecoia \brā´´dē ə koi´yə\ hearing impaired

bradyesthesia \brā´´dē es thē´zhə\ reduced perceptual ability

bradyglossia \brā´´dē glō´sē ə\ abnormally slow speech

bradykinesia \brā´´dē ki nē´zhə\ abnormally slow physical movement; slowness of response

bradylalia \brā´´dē lā´lē ə\ slow speech

bradylexia \brā´´dē lek´sē ə\ slowness in reading that is not related to ignorance, defective vision or mental retardation

bradylogia \brā´´ dē lō´ jē ə\ slowness of speech due to mental disorder

bradyphasia \brā´´dē fā´zhə\ abnormally slow speech due to central nervous system damage

bradyphemia \brā´´dē fē´mē ə\ slowness of activity and response as a result of encephalitis

bradyphrasia \brā´´dē frā´zhə\ slow-

ness of speech due to emotional disorder

bradyphrenia \brā´´dē frē´nē ə\ postencephalitic reduction of interest, motivation and activity

braille \brāl\ reading system for the blind consisting of raised dots that are read by finger touch

brailler \brāl´ėr\ braille writer; a typewriter that types braille

brain \brān\ central nervous system tissue contained within the head

brain damage \brān dam´əj\ structural injury to the brain

brain fever \brān fē´vėr\ inflammation of the brain or its covering; encephalitis

brain injury \brān in´jə rē\ destruction or damage to the tissues of the brain

brain lesion \brān lē´zhən\ localized brain tissue damage

brain stem \brān stem\ brain axis between the cerebrum and the spinal cord, which includes motor and sensory tracts

brainwash \brān wäsh\ to indoctrinate so intensively as to effect a radical transformation of beliefs and attitudes

breathiness \breth´ē nəs\ a speech abnormality characterized by excessive expiration of air

breech delivery \brēch dē liv´ə rē\ condition in which a child is born buttocks first

Broca's aphasics \brō´kəs ə fā´siks\ inability to communicate due to damage of Broca's area in the cortex

bromhidrosis \brōm´´hī drō´sis\ offensive body odor

bromide \brō´mīd\ compounds of bromine, some of which are used as sedatives and anticonvulsant medications

bromism \brō´miz əm\ overdose of bromides

bronchography \bron kog´rə fē\ radiological examination of the lungs

brontophobia \bron´´tō fō´ bē ə\ abnormal fear of lightning and thunder

brushfield spots \brush´fēld spots\ speckling of the iris noted in many cases of Down's syndrome

bruxism \bruk´siz əm\ grinding of teeth, mainly during sleep

buccal \būk´əl\ referring to the cheek

buccal smear \būk´əl smēr\ test employed to study chromatin masses in cells; used to screen for the presence of sex chromosome aberrations

bulimia \bū lim´ē ə\ continuing insatiable appetite for food

bulla \búl´ ə\ large blister

buphthalmos \buf thal´mōs\ morbid enlargement of the eye

bursa \bėr´sə\ fluid filled cavity located so as to reduce friction between body parts

bursitis \bėr sī´tis\ inflammation of a bursa

C **cachexia** \kə kek´sē ə\ general physical deterioration
cacotrophy \ka kô´trə fē\ malnutrition
cadmium \kad´mē um\ metal having an atomic number of 48; its compounds are used in medicine and pain preparation; its salts are poisonous and may constitute an environmental hazard
Caesarean section \si sēr´ē ən sek´shən\ surgical removal of an infant through the abdominal tissue
café au lait \kä´fē ä lā´\ light brown spots of increased skin pigmentation; associated with certain neurocutaneous syndromes
calcification \kal´´si fi kā´shən\ the process in which tissue becomes hardened by deposits of calcium
caligo \kə li´gō\ weakness of vision
callomania \kal´´ō mā´nē ə\ the delusion that one is very goodlooking
calorie \kal´ə rē\ the unit of heat used to measure the energy of food
Calvé-Perthes disease \kav-pėr´thez di zēz´\ crumbling and softening of the head of the femur that fits into hip socket
cancer \kan´sėr\ a malignant, cellular tumor
canthus \kan´thəs\ angle formed where the upper and lower eyelids are joined; the two canthi are referred to as temporal (outer) and nasal (inner)
capacity \kə pas´i tē\ potential ability
carbohydrate \kär´´bō hī´drāt\ various neutral compounds constituting a major part of human food, i.e. sugars, starches and cellulose
carcinogen \kär sin´ə jən\ cancer-producing substance
carcinoma \kär´´sə nō´mə\ cancer; malignancy
carcinophobia \kär´´sin ə fō´bē ə\ irrational fear of having cancer
cardiac \kär´dē ak\ referring to the heart
cardiograph \kär´dē ə graf´´\ instrument used to indicate rate, rhythm and force of the heart
cardioneurosis \kär´´ dē ō nü rō´sis\ emotional disorder characterized by heart palpitations caused by anxiety
cardiovascular \kär´´dē ô vas´kyə lėr\ pertaining to the blood vessels and heart
caries \kār´ēz\ decay of tooth or bone
carpal \kär´pəl\ referring to the wrist
carrel \kär´əl\ a study booth designed to minimize outside stimulation and distraction
carrier \kär´ē ėr\ individual who can transmit but does not manifest a genetic trait
cartilage \kär´tə lij\ elastic, white substance that is attached to the surfaces of the joints and forms certain parts of the skeleton
case history \kās his´tō rē\ a collection of all available data on the previous growth and development of a person or a family
castration complex \kas trā´shən kom´pleks\ fear of genitalia loss; in psychoanalytic terms, refers to a threat to a person's sexuality or sexual role
catabolism \kə tab´ə liz´´ əm\ metabolic process whereby protoplasm is broken down
catalepsy \kat´ə lep´´sē\ symptom of several different psychiatric disorders in which muscles are held rigid for extended periods of time
catalexia \kat´´ə lek´sē ə\ a reading defect in which there is a tendency to reread words and phrases
catalogia \cat´´ə lō´jē ə\ meaningless speech, idiololia
catalyst \kat´ə list\ a substance that alters a chemical process without being changed itself; something that influences a social process without being involved in or altered by the process
cataphasia \kat´´ə fā´zhə\ speech defect in which a person keeps repeating the same words or phrases
cataphoria \kat´´ə fō´ rē ə\ a condition in which the visual axes of both eyes turn downward
cataphrenia \kat´´ə frē´nē ə\ a state of temporary mental confusion

cataract\kat´ə rakt´´\opacity of the lens of the eye that interferes with vision

catarrhal deafness \kə tär´əl def´nəs\ hearing loss due to inflammation of the mucous membrane of the air passages in the head and throat resulting in blockage of the Eustachian tube

catastrophic reaction\kat´´ə strof´ik rē ak´shən\ sudden, severe disintegration of the personality due to stress

catatonia \kat´´ə tō´nē ə\ type of schizophrenia in which the patient is often negativistic, inflexible and given to stereotyped mannerisms.

categorical \ka´´tə gôr´i kəl\ refers to the practice of labeling individuals on the basis of their type of handicap rather than on the basis of educational need

catharsis \kə thär´sis\ process of releasing repressed thoughts in order to reduce tension

cathexis\kə thek´sis\attributing special emotional significance to a person, object, goal or idea; the affective or motivating value of something

causal\kä´səl\ the relationship between cause and effect

cebocephalus \sē´´bō sef´ə lus\ conceptus with a congenital cranial defect characterized by a deformed nose and small closely set eyes

ceiling \sē´ling\ the upper limit of correct test responses

cell\sel\ mass of protoplasm containing a nucleus

cenogenesis \sē´´nō jen´ə sis\ the process in which new characteristics appear in a species due to environmental demands

cenophobia \sē´´ne fō´bē ə\ unusual fear of large open areas

cenotophobia \sē´´nō tō fō´be ə\ dread of change or novelty

central nervous system \sen´trəl nėr´vəs sis´təm\ brain and spinal cord; abbreviated as C. N. S.

centromere\sen´trə mēr´´\nonstaining constriction visible in chromosomes during prophase, metaphase and anaphase

cephalic \sə fal´ik\ referring to the head

cerebellum \sãr´´ə bel´əm\ part of the brain lying behind and above the medulla, involved in muscle coordination and maintenance of body equilibrium

cerebral anoxia \sə rē´brəl ə noks´ē ə\ insufficient supply of oxygen to the brain

cerebral cortex \sə rē´brəl kôr´teks\ outer gray layer that covers the brain

cerebral dominance \sə rē´brəl dom´i nəns\ stronger influence of one side of the brain over the other as manifested by motoric laterality

cerebral lipidosis \sə rē´brəl li´´pi dō´sis\ disorders of lipid metabolism affecting the brain

cerebral palsy \sə rē´ brəl päl´zē\ paralysis or muscular incoordination due to central nervous system maldevelopment or damage

cerebropathy \sãr´´ə brop´ə thē\ brain damage or malfunction

cerebrospinal \sə rē´brō spīn´əl\ pertaining to the brain and spinal cord as in cerebrospinal fluid

cerebrospinal fluid \sə rē´´ brō spī´ nəl flüid\ the fluid within the cranial vault and spinal cord

cerebrotonia \sə rē´´brə tō´nē ə\ personality type characterized by timidity, inhibition and introversion

cerebrum\sə rē´brəm\ main part of the brain, occupying the upper and forepart of the cranial vault; the organ of voluntary control, conscious sensation and learning processes

cerumen\sə rū´ mən\ waxlike secretion found in the external canal of the ear

cervix \sėr´viks\ neck

chaining \chān´ing\ the technique of using the reinforcer of behavior as a stimulus to elicit a second behavior

chalazion \kə la´zē ən\ inflamed enlargement of a small gland of the eyelid

chancre \shang´kėr\ syphilitic sore or lesion

character\kãr´ək tër\total of a person's

behavior patterns, attitudes and methods of coping with life

character disorder \kăr´ək tër dis ôr´dėr\ major defect of personality organization characterized by aggressive acting-out behavior in the absence of anxiety and quiet

characteristic \kâr´´ək tə ris´tik\ typical of person, entity or circumstance

character neurosis \kăr´ək tër nü rō´sis\ disturbance in personality pattern, with or without symptoms

cheilophagia \kē´´lō fā´jē ə\ compulsive biting of one's own lips

cheimaphobia \kē mə fō bē ə\ unusual fear of coldness

chelate \kē´lāt\ to combine with a metal; chelating substances used to remove toxic metals, such as lead from lead poison victims

chemotherapy \kē´´mə thār´ ə pē\ treatment of a disease or condition with chemical agents, such as tranquilizers, anticonvulsants and sedatives

cheromania \kē´´rō mā´nē ə\ mental disorder characterized by euphoria, gaiety and unusual cheerfulness

cherophobia \kē´´rō fō´bē ə\ unusual dread of gaiety

child abuse \chīld ə būs´\ the neglect, negligence, physical or mental injury of a minor by a person legally responsible for the child's welfare

child advocate \chīld ad´və kət\ person or group who seeks legal entitlements on behalf of a child

chiroscope \kī´rə skōp´\ device used in the training of binocular vision; cheiroscope

choleric \kol´ėr ik\ quick tempered; irascible

cholesterol \kə les´tə rôl\ fatty, crystalline alcohol found in all animal fats and oils, important in metabolism

chondrodystrophy \kon´´drō dis´trə fē\ condition characterized by abnormal growth of cartilage

chorea \kō rē´ə\ rapid, jerky, involuntary movements that are a feature of a number of disorders, including cerebral palsy

choreiform movements \kō rē´ə fôrm´´ muv´mənts\ irregularly and arrhythmically spasmodic or jerky movement in different muscles

choreoathetosis \kôr´´ē ō ath´´ə tō´ sis\ a form of cerebral palsy characterized by symptoms consisting of both athetosis and chorea

chorion \kôr´ ē on\ outermost covering of the zygote

chorioretinitis \kō´´rē ō ret´i nī təs\ inflammation of the choroid and retina

choroid \kôr´oid\ vascular covering of the posterior portion of the eyeball

choromania \kôr´´ ə mā´ne ə\ morbid desire to dance

chromatid \krō´mə tid\ one of two spiral, threadlike parts of a chromosome

chromatin \krō´ mə tin\ substance in cell nuclei that stains easily

chromatophobia \krō´´mä tə fō´bē ə\ unusual dislike or aversion to certain colors

chromosome \krō´mə sōm´´\ one of a number of small masses within cells that contains genes and the hereditary instructions for the growth of animals and plants; chromosome count varies between animals with the normal human complement being 46

chromosome error \krō´mə sōm ār´ər\ abnormalities of cell division due to nondisjunctions, translocations or fragmentations that may result in defective offspring

chromosome fragmentation \krō´ mə sōm frag´´mən tā´shən\ chromosome breakage in which parts may become loose, misaligned or translocated

chronic \kron´ik\ pertaining to a condition that progresses and is of long duration

chronological age \kron´´ə loj´i kəl āj\ actual number of years one has lived

cibophobia \sī´´bō fō´bē ə\ morbid dislike of food

cicatrix \sik´ə triks\ scar left by a wound that has healed

ciliary \sil´ē ār´´ē\ referring to the cilia or eyelashes

cilium \sil´ē əm\ eyelash

cineplasty \sin´ə plas´´ tē\ surgical procedure which permits muscles to move prosthetic devices

circulatory system \sër´´kyə la tôr´e sis´təm\ collection of vessels that transmit blood within an animal; cardiovascular system

cirrhosis \si rō´sis \ progressive, inflammatory disease of the liver

clarification \klăr´´i fə kā´shən\ contribution toward ease of understanding

claudication \klä´´di kā´shən\ limping

claustrophilia \kläs´´tro fil´ē ə\ morbid desire to seek security by confining oneself to a small space

claustrophobia \kläs´´tro fō´bē ə\ chronic, unreasonable fear of small, enclosed places

clavicle \klav´i kəl\ collarbone

cleft lip \kleft lip\ incomplete prenatal closure of the upper lip, often in conjunction with cleft palate

cleft palate \kleft pal´ət\ incomplete closure of the two facial halves that may result in such defects as harelip, cleft mandible or cleft soft palate

climacophobia \klī´´mə kō fō´bē ə\ unusual dread of climbing

clinging personality \kling´ing pėr´´sə nal´i tē\ dependent behavior demonstrated when an individual stays near another beyond his or her reasonable needs and the desire of the other person

clinical \klin´i kəl\ observed characteristics or traits

clinical types \klin´i kəl tīps\ persons who possess certain pathological features pronounced enough to classify them in special categories or syndromes

clinic team \klin´ik tēm\ interdisciplinary team that may consist of a psychiatrist, psychologist, social worker and other professional personnel

clinodactyly \klī´´nō dak´tə lē\ short, incurved digits; incurved fifth finger

as frequently noted in Down's syndrome

clone \klōn\ living organism derived asexually from another single organism

clonus \klō´nəs\ rhythmic, rapid alteration of contraction and relaxation of a muscle

closure \klō´zhər\ completion of a behavior or mental act

clubfoot \ klub´fůt\ congenital foot deformity; also called talipes equinovarus

clumbering \klum´ėr ing\ rapid, nervous speech marked by omission of sounds or syllables

cluttering \klu´tėr ing\ rapid, incoherent speech; agitolalia

cochlea \kōk´lē ə\ cone-shaped tube forming a portion of the inner ear; contains the receptors for hearing

codominance \kō dom´ə nəns\ genetic process in which allelic genes are both fully expressed in the heterozygote

cognition \kog nish´ən\ process of knowing

cognitive defect \kog´nə tiv dē´fekt\ perceptual functioning that is inadequate

cognitive learning \kog´nə tiv lėr´ning\ ability to reason abstractly

cognitive style \kog´nə tiv stīl\ the approach used by an individual in problem solving or learning

coitus \kō´i təs\ sexual intercourse

colloquium \kə lō´kwē um\ a type of conference used to plan, evaluate and administer learning experiences or research projects

coloboma \kōl´´ō bō´mə\ congenital cleft or fissure of the eye

colony \kôl´ə nē\ residential institutions for the mentally retarded

color blindness \kul´ėr blīnd´nəs\ inability to distinguish between one or more colors

color coding \kul´ėr kō´ding\ using color on objects or printing in order to facilitate learning

coma \ko´mə\ extended unconsciousness

comatose \kom´ə tōs´´\ being in an unconscious state

combat fatigue \kom´bat fə tēg´\ temporary personality disorganization following the pressure of battle or other stressful situations

combined method \kəm bīnd´ me´ thəd\ the use of both oral and manual procedures in the education of the hearing impaired

commitment \kə mit´mənt\ confinement, treatment or assignment to custody by court order

communicable \kə mūn´i kə bul\ capable of being transmitted from person to person

communitization \kə mūn´´i tī zā´shən\ the process of returning institutionalized persons to the community; deinstitutionalization

compartmentalization \kəm pârt´´men tə lī zā´shən\ the tendency to keep parts distinct that should be considered as a whole; to keep differing moral codes for such life areas as religion, family and business

compensation \kom´´pən sā´shən\ adaptive phenomena in which an area of strength is used to replace, conceal or distract from an area of weakness

compensatory education \kom pen´sə tôr´´ ē ej´´ ū kā´shən\ enriched educational program that attempts to compensate for limited environment

competency test \kom´pi tən sē test\ examination to determine if an individual is capable of unsupervised functioning

competitive personality \kom pe´ti tiv pėr´´sə nal´i tē\ characteristics of a person who feels a need to show superior abilities over others

complex \kom´pleks\ grouping of interrelated factors

comprehension \kom´´pri hen´shən\ level or degree of understanding

comprehensive plan \kom´´pri hen´siv plan\ a legal document outlining an educational agency's prescription of how it intends to meet the needs of its handicapped children

compulsion \kəm pul´shən\ irresistible urge to do or say something contrary to one's common sense or better judgment

conation \kō nā´shən\ the conscious desire to act; the will

concave lenses \kon´cāv lenz´ əz\ corrective eyeglasses in which the surface curves toward the eye; used in the correction of myopia

concept \kon´sept\ picture of something in one's mind

conceptual \kən sep´shü əl\ mental image of an event

conceptualization \kən sep´´shü əl ī zā´shən\ thinking abstractly

conceptual model \kən sep´shü əl mod´əl\ set of assumptions delineating practice or research

conceptus \kən sep´ təs\ the living organism from zygote state to birth

concha \kon´chə\ structure resembling a shell in shape as the auricle of the external ear

concordance \kən kôr´dəns\ in genetics refers to the degree (percentage) of similarity between siblings or other related individuals with regard to specific trait

concrete mode \kon´krēt mōd\ a method of learning characterized by using tangible, real objects and items

concussion \kən kush´ən\ condition caused by a violent blow to the head resulting in loss of consciousness, dizziness, nausea, weak pulse and slow respiration

conditioned reflex \kon di´shənd rē´fleks\ a learned, automatic response to a particular stimulus

conditioning \kən di´shən ing\ the process of developing a relationship between a stimulus and a response

conduction deafness \kən duk´shən def´nəs\ impairment of hearing due to damage or obstruction of the ear canal, drum membrane or the ossicular chain in the middle ear; a failure of air vibrations to be conducted adequately to the cochlea

cones \kōnz\ cell structures within the eye that specialize in color and daytime visual acuity

confabulation \kən fab´´yə lā´shən\ inconsistent falsification of memories

configuration \kən fig´´yə rā´shən\ the relationship between various parts of a thing; the external pattern of an object

configuration clue \kən fig yə rā shən klü\ determining the identity of a word by its general details or pattern

conflict \kon´flikt\ anxiety generated by simultaneous and mutually exclusive or incompatible needs or desires

conformity \kən fôr´mə tē\ adjusting to a social milieu by adopting its rules and standards

confusion \kən fū´zhən\ disturbed orientation in respect to time, place or person, sometimes accompanied by disturbances of consciousness

congener \kon´jə nėr\ one of the same kind or type

congenital \kən jen´i təl\ to be born with

congenital amputation \kən jen´itəl am´´pū tā´shən\ lacking one or both arms, hands or legs at birth

congenital deafness \kən jen´i təl def´nəs\ unable to hear at birth

congenitally blind \kən jen´i tə lē blīnd\ lack of vision, present at birth

conjugation \kon´´jū gā´shən\ the union of sperm and egg; the joining of two separate, distinct entities

conjunctiva \kon´´junk tī´və\ sensitive membrane that covers the anterior portion of the eyeball and also lines the eyelids

conjunctivitis \kən junk´´tə vī´təs\ inflammation of the conjunctiva

connatal \kon nāt´əl\ congenital

consanguinity \kon sang gwin´i tē\ relationship due to common ancestry

conscience \kon´shəns\ self-critical part of one's self in which there are standards of behavior, performance and value judgments

consciousness \kon´shəs nes\ the sum total of awareness

consensual eye reflex \kon sen´shü əl ī rē´ fleks\ contraction of a shaded eye when the other eye is stimulated by light

conservative \kȯn sėr´ və tiv\ favoring little or no change

consonant \kon´sə nənt\ speech sound produced, with or without laryngeal vibration, by certain successive contractions of the articulatory muscles that modify, interrupt or obstruct the expired air stream; excludes all vowels

constant \kon´stənt\ factor that does not vary in size, degree or effect

constituent element \kən stich´ ü ənt el´ə mənt\ ingredient component or part of a whole

constitution \kon´´sti tü´shən\ unity or totality of qualities of an organism

constitutional \kon´´sti tü´shə nəl\ referring to the body

construct \kon´strukt\ a set of ideas composed for theoretical purposes that are usually unobservable

contact lenses \kon´takt lenz´ ez\ eyeglasses that fit directly on the cornea, designed to correct refractive errors

contactology \kȯn´´tak tôl´ ə jē\ the science of contact lenses

contamination \kən tam´´ə nā´shən\ presence of infectious or otherwise dangerous substances in food, water, air, soil or other critical environmental areas

contextual speech \kon teks´chü əl spēch\ interwoven use of the definition of words that explains their meaning

continence \kon´te nəns\ the ability to control passion; ability to control toilet function

contingency \kən tin´jən sē\ relationship between a response and its consequences

contingency management \kən tin´jən sē man´əj mənt\ educational programming in which certain behaviors are altered using reward and punishment appropriately

continuing education \kən tin´ū ing ej´´ū kā´shən\ learning opportunities offered beyond the traditional school programs

continuum \kon tin´ū əm\ the infinite range of values between two values

contraception \kon´trə sep´shən\ method of preventing pregnancy

contraction \kən trak´shən\ drawn together or shortened as in muscle function

contracture \kən trak´chėr\ anatomical deformity caused by prolonged muscle spasticity

control \kən trōl´\ in research, a standard with which experimental observations may be compared

control braces \kən trōl brā´səz\ device used to direct or regulate the movement of a body part

control group \kən trōl´ grüp\ the group that is closely matched with the study group on all important variables except the experimental variable

controlling type \kən trōl´ing tīp\ a dominant personality who has a great need to cause others to submit to his or her will

contusion \kən tü´shən\ bruise

convergence \kən vėr´jəns\ inclination of the axis of vision toward a common point

convergent squint \kən vėr´jənt skwint\ convergent strabismus

convergent strabismus \kən vėr´jənt strə biz´məs\ visual defect in which one eye turns inward toward the other eye

conversion \kən vėr´zhən\ a rapid change in belief from one set of values or attitudes to another

conversion reaction \kən vėr´zhən rē ak´shən\ process in which emotional conflict is reduced by physical symptoms of psychological origin; hysteria

convex lenses \kon´veks lenz´əz\ eyeglasses in which the surface curves away from the eye; used in the correction of hyperopia

convolution \kon vō lü shən\ any of the irregular folds on the exterior surface of the brain

convulsion \kən vul´shən\ forceful, involuntary contractions of voluntary muscles, as in certain types of epileptic seizures

convulsive disorder \kən vul´siv dis ôr´dėr\ condition characterized by convulsions; epilepsy

convulsive therapy \kən vul´siv thăr´ə pē\ shock treatment

coordinates \kō ôr´ di nəts\ points or lines of reference by which objects may be spatially located

coordination \kō´´ôr də nā´ shən\ smooth, harmonious functioning of related parts

coping behavior \kō´ping bē hāv´yėr\ the actions or techniques an individual uses to interact with the environment

copiopia \kōp´´ē ō´pē ə\ eyestrain resulting from overwork or misuse of the eyes

copodyskinesia \kō´´pō dis´´ki nē´zhə\ fatigue and boredom resulting from repetitious work or activity

copracrasia \kōp´´rə krā´zhə\ loss of voluntary control to retain fecal matter

coprolagnia \kop´´rə lag´nē ə\ sexual arousal stimulated by the thought, sight or odor of feces

coprolalia \kop´´rə lā´lē ə\ habitual, obsessive use of obscene language

coprophilia \kop´´rə fēl´yə\ undue interest in feces

coprophobia \kop´´rə fō´bē ə\ morbid fear of feces

copulation \kop´´ū lā´shən\ sexual intercourse

core curriculum \kôr kə rik´yə ləm\ the body of general studies required of all students

cornea \kôr´nē ə\ transparent membrane that covers the forward portion of the eye

corneal graft \kôr´nē əl graft\ surgical procedure that replaces portions of an opaque cornea with transparent cornea in order to improve vision

Cornelia de Lange's syndrome \kôr nēl´yə də lonzh´ sin´drōm\ condition characterized by craniofacial abnormalities, dwarfism, skeletal malformations and mental retardation

coronal \kə rō´nəl\ one of the sutures of the head, premature closure of which may result in acrocephaly

coronary \kôr´´ə năr´ē\ refers to structures such as ligaments or blood vessels arranged in the form of a crown; most commonly refers to the heart's arterial vessels

coronary occlusion \kôr´´ə năr´ē ə klü´zhən\ obstruction of an artery nurturing a portion of the heart

coronary thrombosis \kôr´´ə năr´ē throm bō´sis \ blockage of a heart artery by a blood clot resulting in a heart attack

corrective braces \kôr rek´tiv brā´sez\ devices used to support or straighten body parts

correlation \kôr´´ə lā´shən\ variables, dependently interrelated so that a change in one variable results in a change in the other

cortex \kôr´teks\ outside portion of cerebrum

cortisone \kôr´tə zōn´\ an adrenal hormone used extensively in medical treatment

counseling \koun´sə ling\ a relationship in which one person attempts to help another in such areas as personal adjustment or educational or vocational direction

counterconditioning \koun´tėr kən di´shən ing\ the reduction of an aversive reaction through association of pleasant experiences with that which is feared

covariance \kō văr´ē əns\ the tendency of two variables to change together

coverant behavior \kō´vėr ənt bē hāv´yėr\ inner thoughts or feelings that are controlled by environmental consequences

covert \kō´vėrt\ refers to that which cannot be observed

coxa \kok´sə\ hip, also used to denote hip joint

cranial defect \krā´nē əl dē´fekt\ developmental abnormalities involving

the skull, such as microcephaly and hydrocephalus

craniofacial dysostosis \krān´´ē ō fā´shəl dī´´sə stō´səs\ Crouzon's disease

craniostenosis \krān´´ē ō stə nō´səs\ premature closure of cranial sutures that results in growth deformities

cranium \krān´ē əm\ bony structure of the upper part of the head

cretin \krēt´ən\ person suffering from cretinism

cretinism \krēt´ə niz´´əm\ severe congenital hypothyroidism

cri du chat syndrome \krē dü shot sin´drōm\ chromosome disorder characterized by microcephaly, hypertelorism, mental retardation and a catlike cry in infancy

crisis intervention \krī´sis in´´tėr ven´shən\ emergency service available for those in need of emotional support

criterion \krī tēr´ē ən\ the rule or standard to which comparisons are made

criterion reference \krī tēr´ē ən ref´ėr əns\ evaluation of learning or behavior on the basis of specific, stated goals as opposed to norm reference or comparison with the performance of others

cross categorical \kros ka´´tə gôr´i kəl\ refers to educational programming aimed at including more than one type of handicapped person

crossing over \kros´ing ō´vėr\ exchange of chromatic material between synapsed, homologous chromosomes during prophase of the first meiotic division

Crouzon's disease \krü´zonz di zēz´\ mental retardation syndrome characterized by craniofacial malformations and exophthalmos

cryptogenic \krip´´tə jen´ik\ of unknown origin

cryptorchism \krip tôr´kiz əm\ developmental anomaly in which testes fail to descend into the scrotum; cryptorchidism

crystalline lens \kris´tə lin lenz\ part of

the eye located between the aqueous and vitreous humors that serves to focus light rays on the retina

cubitus valgus \kū´bə təs val´gəs\ defect of the forearm in which it deviates away from the midline when the palm is extended upward

cue \kū\ a sign that stimulates action

cued speech \kūd spēch\ the use of hand signals in association with lip movement in communication with the deaf

cultural familial retardation \kul´chėr əl fə mil´yəl rē´´tär dá´shən\ lower intelligence of unknown origin associated with history of retardation in other family members

culture \kul´chėr\ accepted values, standards, and common life style of a group of people

culture conflict \kul´chėr kon´flikt\ the stress that emerges between differing groups when they come into close approximation

culture-free test \kul´chėr frē test\ evaluation of a person that is designed to minimize or eliminate cultural biases

cumulative record \kūm´ə lə tiv rek´érd\ a continuous written account of a student's behavior and performance

cunnilingus \kun´´ə ling´gəs\ oral stimulation of female genitalia

curriculum \kə rik´yə ləm\ educational program

custodial \kus tō´dē əl\ totally dependent; requiring supervision throughout life

cutaneous \kū tā´ne əs\ refers to the skin

cyanopsia \sī´´ə nop´sē ə\ visual defect characterized by a bluish tinge to all perceptions

cyanosis \sī´´ə nō´səs\ bluish skin coloration; poor oxygenation of the blood

cybernetics \sī´´bėr net´iks\ study of human intellectual functions and their imitation by mechanical and electrical systems

cybertype \sē´bėr tīp\ a typewriter

activated by a remote electronic device used by the severely physically impaired to communicate

cyclitis \si klī´təs\ inflammation of the ciliary body

cyclofusional movement \sī´´klō fū´shən əl müv´ mənt\ rotation of the eyeballs to gain binocular vision

cycloid \sī´kloid\ personality characterized by marked mood variation

cyclophoria \sī´´klō fôr´ē ə\ form of heterophoria in which one eye rotates due to eye muscle imbalance

cyclopia \sī klō´pē ə\ craniofacial defect in which the ocular orbits are fused into one; synophthalmia

cycloplegia \sī´´klō plē´jē ə\ paralysis of the ciliary body of the eyes, which affects accommodation

cycloplegic drug \sī´´klō plēj´ik drug\ drug that dilates the pupil; used to evaluate the nature and degree of refractive error

cyclops \sī´klops\ a fetus with cyclopia

cyclotropia \sī´´klō trō´pē ə\ deviation of the eye around the front to rear axis when fusion is required

cylindrical lenses \si lin´dri kəl lenzes\ eyeglasses designed to correct astigmatism

cymbocephaly \sim´´bō sef´ə lē\ scaphocephaly

cypridophobia \sip´´rid ə fō´bē ə\ morbid dread of contracting venereal disease

cyst \sist\ sac containing fluid or other material

cystic fibrosis \sis´tik fī brō´sis\ a genetic disease involving dysfunction of the exocrine glands resulting in pulmonary, pancreatic and other organ involvement

cytogenetics \sī tō jə net´iks\ branch of genetics that studies the hereditary aspects of genes and chromosomes

cytology \sī tol´ə jē\ study of cells

cytomegalic inclusion disease \sī´´tō mə gal´ik in klü´shən di zez\ viral disease that may result in mental and physical defects in babies

D **dacnomania** \dak´´nō mā´nē ə\ a chronic, unreasonable urge to kill

dacryocystitis \dak´´rē ō sis tī´ təs\ inflammation of the lacrimal sac

dactylology \dak´´tə lol´ə jē\ using the fingers to communicate by sign language

dactylomegaly \dak´´ti lō meg´ə lē\ abnormally large fingers and toes

daltonism \däl´ tən iz əm\ red-green color blindness

Dandy-Walker syndrome\dan´dē wä´ker sin´drōm\ congenital atresia of foramina resulting in hydrocephalus and possible mental retardation

darwinism \där´win iz əm\ theory set forth by Charles Darwin that animals and plants evolve through time due to natural selection

data \dā´tə\ plural of datum; a collection of factual information used for inference and deduction

deaf \def\ unable to hear

deaf-blind \def—blīnd\ a person whose hearing and vision are so impaired that special methods of communication are required

deaf-mute \def-mūt\ unable to speak due to inability to hear

debility \də bil´i tē\ weakness; lack of vigor

decibel \des´ə bel´´\ sound intensity unit of measure

deciduous teeth \dē sid´ ū əs tēth\ a child's first set of teeth that are replaced by permanent teeth; baby teeth

decompensation \dē´´kom pən sā´shən\ personality disorganization due to stress

defecation \def´´ə kā´shən\ releasing the contents of the bowels

defect\dē´fekt\imperfection; failure to function at a normal level

defective \dē fek´tiv\ faulty in design, structure or function; a person who has a defect

defense hostility \di fens´ ho stil´i tē\ tendency, conscious or unconscious, to hurt or attack someone who is feared

defense mechanism \di fens´ mek´ə niz´´əm\ pattern or reaction for avoiding emotional distress and danger

deficiency \di fish´ən sē\ incompleteness or lack

deficit\de´fi sit\ the difference between handicapped and normal functioning

deformity \di fôr´mi tē\ maldevelopment or disfiguration of the body

degeneration \di jen´´ə rā´shən\ lowering of quality or efficiency

dehumanization\dē hū´´mə nī zā´shən\ to divest of individuality; to deprive of normal human rights or attributes

deinstitutionalization \dē´´in sti tü shən əl ī zā´shən\ the practice of returning persons to the community after they have been in the more restrictive environment of a hospital or other type of institution

de Lange's syndrome \də lonzh´əz sin´drōm\ Cornelia de Lange's syndrome

delayed recall \dē lād´ ri kol´\ being able to remember something learned after a time lapse

delayed speech \dē lād´ spēch\ failure of speech to develop at the expected age

deletion \di lē´shən\ loss of genetic material from a chromosome

delinquency \di ling´kwən sē\ antisocial behavior, usually by a minor; juvenile delinquency

deliquium \dē lik´kwē um\ impairment of mental function

delirium \di lēr´ē əm\ state of confusion, incoherence and disorientation caused by illness and fever that may be associated with delusions and/or hallucinations

delirium tremens \de lēr´ē əm trem´ənz\ delirium brought on by acute alcoholism that includes trembling, marked anxiety and hallucinations

delivery model \di liv´er ē mo´dəl\ the administrative plan to extend services to the handicapped

delusion \di lü´zhən\ false belief engendered without appropriate basis and maintained despite contrary evidence

delusions of grandeur \di lü´zhəns uv gran´zhėr\ false sense of extraordinary powers

dementia \di men´shə\ mental and behavioral deterioration

dementia praecox \di men´shə prē´koks\ schizophrenia

demography \di mog´rə fē\ study of human population distributions

demonomania \dē´´mon ō mā´nē ə\ psychiatric impairment in which the patient considers himself possessed by demons

demonophobia \dē´´mon ō fō´bē ə\ fear of demons

demonstration class \dem´ən strā´shən klas\ a group of students used to model teaching procedures for teacher training or research purposes

denasality \dē´´nā zal´i tē\ the quality of the voice when the nasal passages are obstructed, preventing adequate nasal resonance during speech

dendrite \den´drīt\ process of a neuron that mediates nerve impulses in the direction of the cell body

dendrophilia \den´´drō fil´ē ə\ erotic love of trees

denial \dē nī´əl\ refusal to believe or accept; reject as unfounded

dentition \den tish´ən\ development and forming of teeth; type, number and arrangement of teeth

denudative \di nū´də tiv\ habitual, inappropriate removal of clothing

deolepsy \dē´ō lep´´sē\ belief that one is possessed by a god

dependency needs \di pen´dən sē nēds\ infantile needs for loving, mothering, affection, shelter, protection and security; need for narcotics

dependent mentally retarded \di pen´dənt men´təl ē rē tärd´əd\ individuals requiring continual supervision in all aspects of living

depersonalization \dē pėr´´sə nəl i zā´shən\ loss of personal identity

depressant \di pres´ənt\ medical agent that reduces motor and overall functional activity

depression \di presh´ən\ emotional state of dejection and gloominess accompanied by lessened sensitization to environmental stimulation

depressive reaction \di pres´iv rē ak´shən\ pessimistic response to misfortune

deprivation \dep´´rə vā´shən\ absence or loss of environmental factors necessary for maximum physical and mental growth

depth perception \depth pėr sep´shən\ ability to perceive the relative dimension and position of an object

dermatitis \dėr´´mə ti´tis\ inflammation of the skin

dermatoglyphics \dėr mat´ō glif´iks\ study of skin ridges, such as those of fingers, toes, hands and feet

dermatophobia \dėr´´mə tō fō´be ə\ morbid fear of cuts or skin lesions

desensitization \dē´´sen si tī zā´shən\ therapeutic process of reducing anxiety by gradual, repeated exposures to the anxiety-producing object or situation

design \dē zīn´\ the blueprint or schematic representation of something; the preconceived plan, as in research design

desired learner outcome \de zīrd lėr´nėr out´kum\ terminal instructional goals as stated in behavioral terms

despondency \di spon´dən sē\ mental state of discouragement with reduced hope for the future

desquamation \des´´kwə mā´shən\ shedding of dry, flaky skin

deterioration \dē tēr´´ē ə rā´shən\ progressive impairment of mental or physical competence

determination \di tėr´´mi nā´shən\ firm resolve to achieve a goal

determinism \dē tėr´mi niz´´əm\ the theory that a person's destiny is determined by outside forces rather than by one's own volition

detoxification \dē tok´´si fə kā´shən\

removal or reduction of toxic substances, as in treatment of lead poisoning

development \di vel´əp mənt\ sequence of growth, usually from a simple to more complex level

developmental disability \di vel´´əp men´təl dis´´ə bil´ə tē\ handicap that originates during the growth years, such as mental retardation, cerebral palsy and epilepsy

developmental quotient \di vel´´əp men´təl kwō´shənt\ score resulting from tests measuring motor and verbal ability in which a comparison is made between the individual's functioning level and chronological age

deviancy model \dē´vē ən sē mod´əl\ an educational or treatment program that focuses upon reducing the discrepancy between actual performance and expected performance

deviate \dē´vē āt´´\ differ significantly from what is average, normal or standard

deviation \dē´´vē ā´shən\ movement away from normalcy

dexterity \deks tăr´i tē\ skillful motor function of the body

diabetes \dī´ə bē´təs\ a disorder with insulin insufficiency resulting in inability to properly metabolize carbohydrates; increased sugar in blood and urine, and increased thirst, hunger and urination are major signs and symptoms

diabetes insipidus \dī´´ə bē´təs in sip´i dəs\ a metabolic disorder accompanied by great thirst and urination without excess of sugar in blood and urine; marked appetite, physical weakness and emaciation are major signs and symptoms

diabetes mellitus \dī´´ə bē´təs mə lī´təs\ a disease caused by insulin deficiency resulting in inability to properly metabolize carbohydrates with excessive sugar in blood and urine; increased thirst, hunger and urination are cardinal signs and symptoms

diabetic coma \dī´´ə bet´ik kō´mə\ state of unconsciousness due to insulin deficiency, often preceded by drowsiness and stupor

diabetic retinopathy \dī´ə bet´ik ret´´i nop´ə thē\ damage to the eye due to insufficient blood supply of the retina as a result of diabetes

diabolepsy \dī ab´ō lep´´sē\ belief by a person that he is possessed by the devil or that he holds unusual powers

diadochokinesis \dī ad´´ə kō ki nē´sis\ the ability to perform rapid alternating movements of a body part

diagnosis \dī´ag nō´sis\ establishing the nature of a disease or condition

diagnosogenic \dī´´əg nō´´sə jen´ik\ the origin of a defect or behavioral problem due to labeling, as when a child stutters following constant reminders of speech imperfections early in life

diagnostic prescriptive \dī´´əg nos´tik prē skrip´tiv\ describes tests that both delineate the nature of a learning problem and indicate the preferred remediation procedures

dialect \dī´ə lekt\ the customary speech of a specific group of people differentiated by region, social class, ethnicity or culture

Diana complex \dī an´ə kom´pleks\ the repressed desire by a female to be male or to have certain male attributes

diataxia \dī´´ə tak´sē ə\ bilateral ataxia

diathesis \dī ath´ə sis\ predisposition to a particular disease or condition

dichorionic \dī´´kôr ē on´ik\ twin embryos having separate chorions

dichotic audition \di kot´ik ä di´shən\ the simultaneous presentation of a differing stimulus to each ear

dichotomy \di kot´ə mē\ division into two groups

differential diagnosis \dif´´ə ren´shəl dī´´əg nō´sis\ analysis aimed at distinguishing a given case or disorder from other disorders presenting similar symptomatology

differential reinforcement \dif´´ə ren´shəl rē´´in fôrs´mənt\ the systematic rewarding of one behavior to the exclusion of other behaviors

differential threshold \dif´´ə ren´shəl thresh´ōld\ the least difference detectable between two stimulations

digraph \dī´graf\ the combination of two letters to form a single sound as in *sh* or *th*

dilantin \dī lan´tin\ a common anticonvulsant medication; diphenylhydantoin

diopter \dī op´tėr\ unit of measurement used to describe the refractive power of lenses

diotic \dī ot´ik\ affecting both ears

diphthong \dif´thong\ speech sound gliding continuously from one vowel to another within the same syllable

diplegia \dī plē´jē ə\ paralysis on both sides of the body involving all four extremities, with the lower extremities more involved than the upper

diploid \dip´loid\ having the normal two sets of chromosomes within a cell

diplopia \di plō´pē ə\ double vision

dipsomania \dip´´sə mā´nē ə\ chronic use of alcohol to the detriment of the user

directionality \di rek´´shə nal´i tē\ ability to distinguish between right and left, up and down, to and fro

disability \dis´ə bil´i tē\ lack of sufficient mental or physical strength, prowess or coordination

disarticulation \dis är tik´´yə lā´shən\ amputation at the joint

discrimination \di skrim´´ə nā´shən\ process of detecting sensory perception differences

disease \di zēz´\ illness or condition having a distinctive symptomatology

disguised rejection \dis gīzd´ ri jek´shən\ overt appearance of love and concern that masks covert guilt, dislike or other negative emotion

disinhibition \dis in´´i bish´ən\ inability to refrain from responding to stimulation excessively

disintegration \dis´´in tə grā´shən\ loss of unity or organization; the falling apart or separation of related parts

disjunction \dis junk´shən\ the separation of parts

dislocation \dis´´lō kā´shən\ displacement of bones or organs from the original location

disorder \dis ôr´dėr\ state of physical or mental defect

disorganization \dis ôr´´gən ī zā´shən\ reduction of smooth, orderly relations between individual components of an organism or system

disorientation \dis ôr´´ē ən ta´shən\ confusion with regard to person, place or time

dispersion \dis pėr´zhən\ the scattering of observations; spreading out from a central location

displacement \dis plās´mənt\ transfer of an affect from one person, place, object or situation to another

dissociation \di sō´sē ā´shən\ lack of ability to see things as a whole

distal \dis´təl\ away from the center; peripheral

distortion \di stôr´shən\ an articulatory defect in speech in which sounds are changed

distractibility \di strakt´´ə bil´i tē\ inability to maintain a normal attention span due to the impingement of irrelevant stimuli

distribution \dis´´tri bū shən\ the grouping of data into categories according to a system; the rate of occurrence of something within specified parameters

diuretic \di´´yə ret´ik\ a food or drug that stimulates urination

diurnal \di ėr´nəl\ happening during daytime

divergent squint \di vėr´jənt skwint\ divergent strabismus

divergent strabismus \di vėr´jənt strə biz´məs\ exotropia; a visual defect in which one eye turns outward from the other eye

dizygotic \dī zī got´ik\ refers to twins originating from different fertilized eggs

dolichocephalic \dol´´i kō sə fal´ik\ having a long head

domatophobia \dō´´mə tō fō´bē ə\

chronic, unreasonable fear of being in a house

dominance \dom´i nəns\ taking precedence; being more important or prominent

dominant gene \dom´ə nənt jēn\ refers to a gene that produces its effect in the presence of a contrasting gene

dormant stage \dôr´mənt stāj\ period during which a disease may be or appear to be asymptomatic

doromania \dôr´´ə mā´nē ə\ unreasonable desire to give presents

dorsal \dôr´səl\ refers to the back of a part

double vision \ du´bəl vi´zhən\ diphopia; the seeing of one object as two

doubling dose \dub´ling dōs\ amount of radiation necessary to double the spontaneous mutation rate

Down's syndrome \dounz sin´drōm\ mental retardation syndrome associated with additional chromosome 21 material; mongolism

doxogenic \dok´´sō jē´nik\ caused by one's own thoughts and feelings; psychogenic; of psychological origin

drapetomania \drap´´ə tō mā´nē ə\ the constant, unreasonable desire to wander from home

drive \drīv\ persistent urge to engage in certain patterns of behavior

dromomania \drō´´mō mā´nē ə\ an unusually strong desire to roam

dromophobia \drō´´mō fō bē ə\ unreasonable fear of running; fear of haste

Drosophila \dro sof´i lə\ fruit fly

drug \drug\ chemical agent used for medicinal purposes or taken to produce a desired physical or mental effect

drug therapy \drug thǎr´ə pē\ use of drugs to treat disease, modify behavior or to enhance learning

drum membrane \drum mem´brān\ substance that separates the external ear from the middle ear

Duchenne's disease \dü´shenz di zēz´\ common type of muscular dystrophy

due process \dü pro´ses\ guarantee of opportunity to present one's position

prior to governmental or educational agency action

dullard \dul´ėrd\ archaic term for slow learner

dull-normal \dul—nôr´məl\ functioning at the lower end of the average range of intelligence

dumb \dumb\ mute

dwarfism \dwôr´ fiz əm\ developmental defect characterized by much less than normal size for a species

dynamometer \dī´´ nə mom´ə ter\ an apparatus that measures muscular strength

dysacousis \dis´´ə kū´sis\ difficulty in understanding speech due to neurological dysfunction

dysarthria \dis är´thrē ə\ deficiency in the normal use of the speech organs

dysarthrosis \dis´´är thrō´sis\ defect or deformity of a joint

dysbasia \dis bā´zhə\ defect in balance, posture and motor coordination; ataxia

dysbulia \dis bü´lē ə\ defect of concentration; extreme distractibility

dyscephaly \dis sef´ə lē\ defect in formation of craniofacial bones

dyscrasia \dis krā´zhə\ abnormal condition, disease or malfunction of the body

dysdiadochokinesia \dis´´dī ə dō´´kō kə nē´sē ə\ defective ability to perform alternative movements

dyseneia \dis´´ə nā´yə\ speech defect due to hearing deficiency

dysesthesia \dis´´es thē´zhə\ abnormally high sensitivity to pain

dysfluency \dis flü´ən sē\ speech marked by hesitations and poor rhythm

dysfunction \dis funk´shən\ abnormality of function or operation of an organ, part or system

dysgenesis \dis jen´ ə sis\ biologically defective, deficient or abnormal

dysgenics \dis jen´iks\ study of factors that cause defective offspring

dysgnosia \dis nō´zhə\ intellectual malfunction

dysgraphia \dis graf´ē ə\ impairment in

ability to write due to central nervous system abnormality

dyskinesia \dis´´ki nē´zhə\ defect in voluntary movement; seizures

dyslalia \dis lā´lē ə\ speech impairment due to tongue or other speech organ abnormalities

dyslexia \dis lek´sē ə\ impairment in the ability to read due to central nervous system abnormality

dyslogia \dis lōj´ē ə\ impairment in thought processes

dysmelia \dis mē´le ə\ malformation of extremities due to interference in embryonic development

dysmenorrhea \dis´´men ə rē´ ə\ painful or difficult menstruation

dysmetria \dis me´trē ə\ inability to control the power and speed of an act to judge properly the distance involved

dysmnesia \dis nē´zhē ə\ impaired memory

dysmorphobia \dis´´môr fō´bē ə\ chronic, unreasonable fear of becoming deformed

dysnomia \dis nō´mē ə\ difficulty in remembering a familiar name

dysopia \dis ō´pē ə\ defective vision

dyspepsia \dis pep´sē ə\ imperfect digestion

dysphagia \dis fā´jē ə\ difficulty in swallowing or inability to swallow

dysphasia \dis fā´zhə\ impairment in speech due to central nervous system pathology

dysphemia \dis fē´mē ə\ speech disorder due to psychogenic origin

dysphonia \dis fŏn´ ē ə\ defect of vocal function

dysphoria \dis fôr´ē ə\ chronic state of anxiety and hyperactivity

dysphrenia \dis frē´nē ə\ a functional psychosis

dysplasia \dis plā´zhə\ developmental abnormality

dyspnea \disp nē´ ə\ abnormal breathing

dyspraxia \dis prak´sē ə\ reduced ability to perform smooth, coordinated movements on request

dysrhythmia \dis rith´mē ə\ defect or disturbance in rhythm

dystaxia \dis tak´sē ə\ partial ataxia

dysthymia \dis thē´mē ə\ tendency to be dejected or despondent

dystonia \dis tō´nē ə\ abnormal muscle tone

dystrophy \dis´trə fē\ defect resulting from a nutritional disorder

dysuria \dis ūr´ē ə\ painful or difficult urination

E **ear canal** \ēr kə nal\ external auditory passage

ecdemomania \ek´´dē mō mā´nē ə\ compulsive desire to wander away from home

echographia \ek´´ō graf´ē ə\ neurological condition in which a person can copy writing but is not able to write for communication purposes

echolalia \ek´´ō lā´lē ə\ echoic speech in which individual repeats sounds or words without meaning or purpose

echopathy \ē kop´ə thē\ the excessive, inappropriate imitation of the actions, gestures, and speech of others

echopraxia \ek´´ō prak´sē ə\ repetition of gestures and actions of others; the meaningless continuation of movements initiated by others

eclampsia \ē klamp´ sē ə\ convulsions and coma in a pregnant woman related to hypertension and edema

eclectic \i klek´tik\ selecting the best features of differing theories or practices

ecmnesia \ek nē´zhə\ a senility symptom in which recent events are difficult to recall, but more remote events can be remembered in great detail

ecobehavioral \ē´´kō bē hāv´yėr əl\ refers to simultaneous consideration of a person and his or her environment with regard to assessment, learning and intervention

ecological model \ek´´ə loj´ i kəl mod´əl\ theory based upon the assumption that behavior disorders are primarily the result of maladaption to the social environment

ecological niche \ek´´ə loj´i kəl nich\ environmental parameters within which an organism functions

ecology \e kol´ə jē\ study of interaction between living organisms and their environment

ecomania \ē´´kō mā´nē ə\ personality type that relates to authority figures with great deference while relating to others (children, employees, etc.) in a very strict, domineering fashion

ecosystem \ek´ō sis´´təm\ interaction between living organisms and their environment

ectomorph \ek´tə môrf´´\ thin person

ectopia \ek tō´pē ə\ abnormal position of an organ or body part

ectropion \ek trō´pē ən\ curling of the eyelid, exposing the conjunctiva

eczema \ek zē´mə\ condition of the skin characterized by itching, redness, weeping lesions and crusting

edema \i dē´mə\ excessive fluid localized in tissue

educable mentally retarded \ej´ū kə bəl men´təl ē rē tärd´əd\ individuals in the upper range of retardation who may have some potential for mastery of academic skills

educationally retarded \ej´´ü kā shə nəl ē re tärd´ əd\ functioning below grade level expectancy

Edward's syndrome \ed´wėrdz sin´drōm\ condition related to a trisomy of chromosome 18 that is characterized by microcephaly, mental retardation and numerous other developmental defects

efferent \ef´ėr ənt\ conducting from a central to a peripheral region, as nerves convey motor impulses from the central nervous system to the muscles

effete \ef fēt´\ exhausted; worn out; no longer capable of producing

ego \ē´go\ self; that part of the personality that mediates one's needs and perceptions of reality

egocentric \ē´´gō sen´trik\ self-centered; preoccupied with one's self

egoist \ē´gō ist\ self-centered person

egomania \ē´´gō mā´nē ə\ abnormal preoccupation with one's self

egosyntonic \ē´´gō sin tō´nik\ harmonious with ego standards

egotism \ē´gō tiz´´əm\ excessive pride and selfishness

eidetic imagery \ī det´ik im´əj rē\ exact recall of visual images; sometimes called photographic memory

elation \ē lā´shən\ strong feeling of well-being and satisfaction

elective mutism \ē lek´tiv mū´tiz əm\ circumstance in which an individual, who is physically able to talk, refuses to speak

Electra complex \i lek´trə kom´pleks\ sexual desire or excessive emotional attachment of a daughter for her father

electroencephalogram \i lek´´trō en sef´ə lə gram´\ graphic record of brain waves (EEG)

electroencephalography \e lek´´trō en sef´´ə log´rə fē\ science of recording and studying the implications of electric currents emitted by the brain; often referred to as EEG recordings

elision \i li´zhən\ the omission of certain speech sounds

ellipsis \i lip´sis\ the omission of a word or words from a sentence that are necessary for complete comprehension of the sentence's meaning

embolus \em´bə ləs\ blood clot in a vessel

embryo \em´brē ō´\ unborn human being from conception until two months; after two months and until birth the term fetus is used

emesis \em´ə sis\ vomiting

emetatrophia \ē´´met ə trō´fē ə\ wasting and weakness due to persistent vomiting, as in, for example, anorexia nervosa

emmetropia \em´´ə trō´pē ə\ perfect vision; a situation where light rays fall in perfect focus on the retina

emote \ē mōt´\ to make an emotional utterance

emotion \ē mō´ shən\ a subjective feeling, as of fear, anger, love, grief

emotional blocking \i mō´shə nəl blok´ing\ inability to make responses as a result of excessive emotion

emotional disturbance \i mō´shə nəl dis tėr´bəns\ mental illness or imbalance

emotional involvement \i mō´shən əl in volv´mənt\ dual relationship on the part of the counselor, that of participant-observer

emotional lability \i mō´shə nəl lə bil´i tē\ tendency toward sudden, unex-

plainable changes in emotional behavior

emotional restriction \i mō´shə nəl rē strik´shən\ characteristic of a person whose feelings are inhibited or limited

emotive \i mō´tiv\ situation that excites or stimulates emotion or feeling

empathy \em´pə thē\ ability to identify with the problems or difficulties of another individual

emphysema \em´´fi sē´mə\ impairment of the lung with distension of the alveoli (lung sacs) with trapped air and resultant respiratory weakness

empirical construct \em pēr´i kəl kon´strukt\ a hypothesized relationship based upon observable data

empirical data \em pēr´i kəl dā´tə\ information based on experience rather than research inferences

empirical sufferance \em pēr´i kəl suf´ə rəns\ passive permission resulting from a dependence upon experience or observation alone, not scientific or theoretical

encephalitis \en sef´´ə lī´tis\ inflammation of the brain

encephalitis lethargica \en sef´ə lī´tis lə thär´ji kə\ sleeping sickness

encephalocele \en sef´ə lō sēl´\ herniation of the brain

encephalography \en sef´´ə log´rə fē\ roentgenographic examination of the brain

encephalomyelitis \en sef´´ə lō mī´´ə lī´tis\ inflammation of spinal cord and brain due to infection

encephalomyelopathy \en sef´´ə lō mī´´ə lop´ə thē\ disease or condition affecting the spinal cord or brain

encephalopathy \en sef´´ə lop´ə thē\ brain damage

encopresis \en´´kō prē´sis\ fecal incontinence

enculturation \en´´kul chėr ā´shən\ the adaptation to a culture; the adoption of a different culture

endemic \en dem´ik\ consistently occurring within a given area

endocrine glands \en´də krin glanz\ glands that secrete substances into the blood that have a characteristic effect on other organs

endogenous \en doj´ə nəs\ originating from within as opposed to exogenous or external origin

endolymph \en´dō limpf\ labyrinthian fluid of the inner ear

endomorph \en´dō môrf\ person with rounded or fat body type

endophasia \en´´dō fā´zhə\ formation of words by lips without producing sound

endophthalmitis \en´´dof thal mī´tis\ inflammation of internal eye tissue

engram \en´gram\ durability of memory

enomania \ē´´nō mā´nē ə\ the persistent craving for alcoholic beverage as a result of alcoholism

enophthalmos \en´´of thal´mōs\ abnormal retroposition of the eye within its orbit

entoptic \en top´tik\ within the eye

entropion \en trō´ pē ən\ curling inward of the margin of the eyelid and eyelashes

enucleation \i nü´klē ā´ shən\ surgical removal of the eyeball

enuresis \en´´yə rē´sis\ bedwetting

environment \en vī´rən mənt\ totality of all conditions and factors in the surroundings of a person, animal or plant

environmentalism \en´´vī rən men´´tə liz´əm\ the view that environment is a more important behavioral detriment than heredity

enzygotic twins \en´´ zī got´ik twinz\ identical twins; genetically identical siblings resultant from a single, fertilized egg

enzyme \en´zīm\ biochemical substance that serves to stimulate change in other substances

epicanthic fold \ep´´ə kan´thik fōld\ vertical fold of skin in the corner of the eye next to the nose; epicanthus

epidemiology \ep´´i dē´´mē ol´ə jē\ study of the relationship between relevant factors in the environment and geographical distribution of a disease or condition

epiglottis \ep i glôt´tis\ the structure that covers the entrance to the larynx

epilepsy \ep´ə lep´´ sē\ seizure or convulsive disorder

epileptic fugue \ep´´ə lep´tik fūg\ period of confusion or reduced awareness that may follow an epileptic seizure

epileptiform \ep´´ə lep´tə fôrm´\ resembling the characteristics of epilepsy; epileptoid

epileptogenic \ep´´i lep tō´jen ik\ able to induce seizure activity

epiloia \ep´´ə loi´yə\ tuberous sclerosis

epiphora \ē pif´ə rə\ excessive tear production due to malfunction of the lacrimal system

epiphysis \e pif´i sis\ end portion of a long bone

epistasis \i pis´tə sis\ process of a gene at one locus suppressing the action of another gene at a different locus

Erb´s palsy \ėrbz pôl´zē\ upper arm type of brachial palsy due to involvement of fifth and sixth cervical nerve roots at birth; Erb-Duchenne paralysis

ergasiomania \ėr ga´´sē ō mā´nē ə\ unusually strong desire to work constantly

ergasiophobia \ėr ga´´sē ō fō´bē ə\ unusually strong aversion to work

erogenous \i roj´ə nəs\ causing feeling of eroticism

erotic \i rot´ik\ pertaining to sexual stimulation

eroticism \i rot´i siz´´əm\ sexual excitement

erotism \ăr´ə tiz´´əm\ eroticism

erotomania \ə rot´´ ə mā´nē ə\ abnormal preoccupation with thoughts about sex; overreaction to sexual stimulation

erythroblast \i rith´rə blast´\ nucleated cell from which red blood corpuscles develop

erythroblastosis \i rith´´rō bla´stō sis\ hemolytic anemia

erythroblastosis fetalis \i rith´rō bla´ stō sis fə tal´is\ damage to the fetus caused by Rh factor incompatibility

esophageal voice \ə sof´ə jē´´əl vois\

low frequency vibrations produced by the upper narrow portion of the esophagus when swallowed air bubbles are emitted

esophoria \es´´ō fôr´ē ə\ type of heterophoria in which the eyes tend to turn inward when fusion is disrupted

esotropia \es´´ə trō´pē ə\ convergent strabismus; eye defect in which one eye turns sharply inward toward the other eye

estrogen \es´trə jən\ one of the female sex hormones

ethics \eth´iks\ the principles that govern conduct

ethology \ē thol´ə jē\ study of animal behavior; also, the study of ethics

ethos \eth´ōs\ the traditional or characteristic outlook of a particular group or culture

etiology \ē´´tē ol´ə jē\ the study of causes of diseases and morbid conditions

eugenics \ū jen´iks\ study of ways to improve the hereditary characteristics of a population

eunuch \ū´nək\ castrated male individual

eunuchoid \ū´nə koid´´\ resembling a eunuch in body configuration

euphoria \ū fôr´ē ə\ exaggerated feeling of well-being

euploidy \ū ploi´dē\ state in which there is a balanced set of chromosomes

eustachian tube \ū stā´shē ən tūb\ canal connecting middle ear to the pharynx

euthanasia \ū´´thə nā´zhə\ painless putting to death of persons suffering from incurable diseases; also called mercy killing

euthenics \ū then´iks\ science dealing with environmental manipulation in order to improve the human race

evaluation \ē val´´ū ā´shən\ appraisal

eversion \ē vėr´zhən\ turning outward

exacerbation \ig zas´´ėr bā´shən\ increase in the severity or seriousness of a disease or condition

exceptional \ek sep´shə nəl\ deviation from the norm or average

exceptional child \ek sep´shə nəl chīld\ individual who is different from the average to the extent that he or she needs special educational provisions

excessive assurances \ek ses´iv ə shėr´ən səs\ promises to improve behavior that are unrealistic

exhibitionism \ek´´sə bish´ə niz´´əm\ exposure of one's body for the purpose of arousing sexual interest in self or others

exogenous \ek soj´ə nəs\ originating externally; opposite of endogenous

exophoria \ek´´sō fôr´ē ə\ type of heterophoria in which the eyes turn outward when fusion is disrupted

exophthalmic goiter \eks´´ of thal´mik goi´tėr\ enlarged thyroid accompanied by protuberant eyes, fatigue and emotional instability

exophthalmos \ek´´sof thal´mōs\ abnormal protusion of the eyeball

exotropia \ek´´sō trō´pē ə\ deviation of one eye away from the other eye so that both eyes cannot focus on an object simultaneously

experiment \ek spēr´ə mənt\ scientific procedure undertaken in order to demonstrate or discover truth

expiration \eks´´pi rā´shən\ breathing out; death

exploitative type \ek sploi´tə tiv tīp\ one who uses others in order to accomplish own goals

expressitivity \ek´´spre si tiv´i tē\ degree to which a genetic trait is manifested

expressive aphasia \ek spre´siv ə fāz´zhə\ disturbance of speech due to brain lesion in which the major difficulty is inability to remember the pattern of movements required to produce words even though the patient knows what he wants to say

extensor \ek sten´sėr\ muscle that straightens or extends a joint

extinction \ek stingk´shən\ progressive reduction or weakening of a conditioned response

extirpation \eks´´tėr pā´shən\ surgical removal of a body part

extrapunitive \eks´´trə pū´nə tiv\ tendency to direct hostility outward, away from self

extrapyramidal system \eks´trə pi ram´ə dəl sis´təm\ system associated with neural activity of frontal cortex and basal nuclei and governing fine motor coordination; functions with pyramidal system

extrinsic motivation \eks trin´sik mō´´ti vā´shən\ behavior controlled through external events rather than inner satisfaction or dissatisfaction

extrinsic muscles \ek strin´sik mus´əls\ external muscles of the eye that control eyeball movement

extrovert \eks´trō vért´\ outgoing person; one who focuses on external interests

eyedness \īd´nəs\ eye dominance; preference to use one eye over the other with respect to sighting or fixating upon objects

eye fixation \i fik sā´shən\ ability to control eye movement accurately

eye ground \ī ground\ fundus; the back of the eye that can be inspected through an ophthalmoscope

eye span \i span\ amount of material, usually letters or numbers, that can be perceived in one fixation of the eyes

eye strain \ī strān\ discomfort of the eyes, usually associated with refractive error, poor lighting or overuse

F

fabrication \fab´ri kā´shən\ deception; falsehood; something that is fabricated or made up

facies \fā shē ēz´´\ medical term for face

facioplegia \fā´´shē ō plē´jē ə\ facial paralysis

factor \fak´tėr\ in biology, a gene, allele or other hereditary determiner

factor analysis \fak´tėr ə nal´ə sis\ method of correlation research to identify and evaluate the main or relevant factors

facultative \fak´əl tā´´tiv\ flexibility in behavior; opposite of obligatory

faculty \fak´əl tē\ any normal function; the professors of a college or university

fading \fād´ing\ an operant conditioning technique in which external reinforcement is gradually reduced

falling sickness \fâl´ing sik´nəs\ epilepsy

Fallopian tube \fə lō´pē ən tūb\ tube connecting egg sac to the uterus

fallout \fäl´out\ the particles produced by a nuclear explosion; the settling to earth of these particles

false labor \fäls lā´bėr\ irregular uterine contractions that do not precipitate birth

falsetto \fäl set´ō\ artificial voice of the male placing it above natural range

familial \fə mil´yəl\ relating to hereditary cause

family tree \fam´ i lē trē\ a chart that graphically depicts family lineages

fanaticism \fə nat´i siz´´əm\ extreme enthusiasm for a cause

fantasy \fan´tə sē\ make believe; the forming of mental pictures; imagination

faradization \fār´´ə dī zā´shən\ therapeutic use of electrical current to stimulate muscles and nerves

farsightedness \fär sī´tid nəs\ hyperopia

father figure \fä´thər fig´yər\ a male adult in authority to whom a person relates as though he were his own father; father image

fauces \fô´sez\ opening leading from mouth to the pharynx

febrile \fē´brīl\ feverish

febriphobia \fēb´´ri fō´bē ə\ anxiety associated with body temperature increase

fecal \fē´kəl\ pertaining to feces

feces \fē´sēz\ stool; excrement

feckless \fek´ləs\ helpless, weak, spiritless

fecund \fē´kund\ productive

fecundity \fe´kun di tē\ productiveness, fertility

feeblemindedness \fē´bəl mīn´did nəs\ term commonly used in the past to denote mental retardation

feedback \fēd´bak\ a process by which a person becomes aware of the nature or quality of certain of his behaviors

fellatio \fə lā´shē ō´´\ oral stimulation of male genitalia

felt-need \felt nēd\ a need of which one is conscious

feminization \fem´´i nī zā´shən\ the induction or appearance of female secondary sex characteristics in a male

femur \fē´mėr\ thigh bone

fenestration \fen´´i strā´shən\ operation that creates an artificial opening into the labyrinth of the ear

feral child \får´əl chīld\ literally, a wild child; one reared without benefit of opportunities for socialization and acculturation

ferric chloride test \får´ik klôr´īd test\ procedure used in screening for phenylketonuria

fertile \fėr´təl\ capable of conceiving

fertilization \fėr´´ti li´zā shən\ the union of sperm and ovum

festination \fes´´ti nā´shən\ a hurrying gait, an involuntary symptom of some nerve diseases

fetal \fēt´əl\ having to do with a fetus

fetalism \fē´təl iz əm\ outdated term for Down's syndrome

feticide \fē´ti sīd\ killing of a fetus

fetishism \fe´ tish iz əm\ sexual excitement or gratification produced by inanimate objects

fetus \fē´təs\ unborn human being

from two months until birth; also spelled foetus

fever blister \fē′vėr blis′tėr\ herpes simplex; a sore on the face often accompanying a cold or a fever

fibril \fī′bril\ a threadlike filament in the body

fibrillation \fī′brə lā′shən\ a pathological condition in which muscular fibrils quiver out of control

fibroma \fī brō′mə\ type of tumor

fibromatosis \fī′′brō mə tō′sis\ the tendency to form fibromas

fibroplasia \fī′′brə plā′ zhē ə\ fibrous tissue formation

fibula \fib′ū lə\ smaller of the two leg bones

field of vision \fēld uv vi′zhən\ total area that can be seen by the eyes without movement or scanning

figure-ground relation \fig′ yėr— ground rē lā′shən\ seeing an object clearly against a background

filial \fil′ē əl\ having to do with offspring or progeny

filiate \fil′ē āt\ legally, to establish paternity; in psychology, to form a parent/child relationship

finger agnosia \fing′gėr ag nō′zhə\ inability or lessened ability to use the sensitivity of the fingers to identify objects handled while blindfolded

finger reading \fing′gėr rēd′′ing\ use of the fingers to read braille

finger spelling \fing′gėr spel′ing\ the forming of letters or sound symbols with the fingers; a type of communication used by the blind

first aid \fėrst ād ̀\ emergency medical care administered before professional help can be obtained

fissure \fish′ėr\ narrow opening

fistula \fis′chə lə\ passage or tube, often leading to an internal hollow organ

fit \fit\ convulsion

fix \fiks\ (slang) shooting heroin into a vein

fixate \fik′sāt\ to become psychologically arrested at an immature stage of development

fixated response \fik′sā təd ri spons ̀\ a response that is not readily altered by reward or punishment

fixation \fik sā′shən\ directing the vision so that the image of the object falls directly on the fovea; in psychological terms, an obsessive or unhealthy attachment

flaccid \flak′sid\ weak or lax; having defective muscle tone

flaccid paralysis \flak′sid pə ral′i sis\ loss of tone; absence of reflexes in affected parts

flagellation \flaj′′ə lā′shən\ the act of whipping or being whipped for religious or aberrant sexual purposes

flagellomania \fla′′jə lō mā′ nē ə\ sexual pleasure obtained from flagellation

flare-up \flãŕ up\ a sudden recurrence of a disease or other condition

flattening of affect \fla′tə ning uv a′fekt\ low or absent emotionality

flexibility \fleks i bil′i tē\ in psychology, the state of being amenable to change; adaptability; easily bent, as a body limb

flexion \flek′shən\ bending of a joint caused by the contraction of muscles crossing the joint, usually a bending towards the ventral side

flexor \flek′sėr\ muscle that flexes or bends a joint

floaters \flō′tėrs\ small particles of cells that move about in the vitreous of the eye

flooding \flud′ing\ desensitization technique in which the patient is continually confronted with the anxiety-producing stimulus

fluency \flü′ən sē\ smooth speech or writing flow

flux \fluks\ abnormally large discharge from the bowels

focal length \fō′kəl length\ eye to object distance

focal lesion \fō′kəl lē′zhən\ injury confined to a particular area

focus \fō′kəs\ point at which rays converge after passing through lens; also, in vocal production, location of tone placement

folie \fō lē´\ French for one who suffers from delusions; mania; psychosis

folie a deux \fo lē´ ə dü\ paired psychoses, as when a husband's and wife's psychiatric impairments are interrelated

follow-up \fôl´ō up\ reexamination of material in the light of new developments

fonator \fō´nā tėr\ electrical device that translates speech into vibrations as a learning aid with the hearing impaired

fontanel \fon´tə nel´\ opening between the cranial bones covered by a membranous tissue; present in the skull of a fetus and infant

food chain \füd chān\ in ecology, an interrelationship of organisms that feed on one another

foofarow \fü´fə rō´´\ overemphasis on trivia

foramen \fō rā´mən\ short passage or orifice, as in a bone

foramen magnum \fō ra´mən mag´nəm\ the large opening at the base of the skull that connects the cranial vault and the vertebral canal

forceps \fôr´seps\ surgical instrument often used in delivery to assist in removing the fetus from the birth canal

foreskin \fôr´skin\ penis skin fold removed in circumcision

formication \fôr´´mi kā´shən\ a tactile feeling, as of crawling ants

fornication \fôr´´ni kā´shən\ sexual intercourse outside of marriage

fornix \fôr´niks\ loose fold; conjunctiva where tissue covering the eyeball and the eyelid meet; any arched structure in the body

fortran \fôr´tran\ a type of computer language

forward chaining \fôr´wėrd chān´ing\ teaching technique in which the behavior to be learned is divided into steps and then taught sequentially from first to last

foundling \found´ling\ an abandoned child

fovea \fō´vē ə\ a pit or cuplike depression

fovea centralis \fō´vē ə sen trā´ lis\ point in the center of the macula where vision is the keenest

fracture \frak´chėr\ break in or of bone

fragilitas ossium \frə jil´i təs os´ē um\ abnormal brittleness of bones

fragmentation \frag´´men tā´shən\ in psychology, the state of disintegration in which a personality functions as though broken into separate parts; disassociation

frame of reference \frām uv ref´ėr əns\ the set of intellectual, emotional and moral constructs with which persons or society perceive and deal with their environment

frantic \fran´tik\ frenzied; wildly excited; archaic for insane

fraternal twins \frə tėr´nəl twinz\ those who develop in the same uterus from separate ova

free association \frē ə sō´´sē ā´shən\ spontaneous reporting of every thought as it comes into the conscious

free-floating anxiety \frē-flō´ting ang zī´i tē\ anxiety that is not related to any particular source

free will \frē wil\ the doctrine that supposes an individual's ability to make voluntary choices; opposite of determinism

frenetic \frə net´ik\ frenzied; wild

frenum \frē´nəm\ fold of skin or mucous membrane that checks or limits the movements of an organ or part, usually the lingual frenum under the tongue

frequency \frē´kwən sē\ with reference to hearing, the term is used to denote the cycles per second of sound waves; in statistics, the term refers to the number of observed occurrences

frequency distribution \frē´kwən sē dis´´tri bū´shən\ a record of the number of times observations are noted at different levels or values

Freudianism \froi´dē an´´iz əm\ the psychoanalytical doctrine proposed by Sigmund Freud; used popularly to explain behavior as sexually motivated

fricative \frik´ə tiv\ speech sound produced by forcing air stream through a narrow opening, resulting in audible high frequency vibrations

Friedreich's disease \frē´driks di´zēz\ familial or hereditary ataxia with early onset

frigid \fri´jəd\ one who is sexually unresponsive or cold; averse to sexual intercourse

frigidity \fri jid´i tē\ limited ability to experience sexual gratification

Fröhlich's syndrome \frā liks sin´drōm\ condition characterized by obesity, short stature and sexual infantilism due to pituitary dysfunction; hypopituitarism; adiposogenital syndrome

frontal lobe \frun´təl lōb\ the forward part of each cerebral hemisphere of the brain

frottage \frô tāzh´\ sexual arousal by rubbing a person of the opposite sex, associated with irresistible impulse of pressing up behind someone in a crowd, thus inducing an orgasm

fructosemia \frük´´tō sē´mē ə\ hereditary disorder to which fructose cannot be properly metabolized causing poor growth and mental retardation if untreated

frustration \frus trā´shən\ nongratification of needs and wants due to obstacles

frustration tolerance \frus trā´shən tol´ėr əns\ the capacity to handle having one's goals blocked

fugue \fūg\ state of amnesia in which memory of past events is impaired but habits and skills previously acquired remain functionable

full-term \fül—tėrm\ denoting a pregnancy in which the baby is born at the completion of its normal intrauterine development

function \funk´shən\ normal performance or operation of a body part, organ system or machine

functional defect \funk´shən´´əl dē´fekt\ deficit without a known organic cause

functional disorder \fünk´shən əl dis ôr´dėr\ problem of function rather than structure, behavioral as opposed to physical

functional retardation \funk´shən əl rē´´tär dā´shən\ limited functioning without evidence of organic defect

fundus \fun´dəs\ back or base of an organ or part furthest from entrance in a hollow organ

fungicide \fun´ji sīd\ a chemical that destroys fungi

furor epilepticus \fūr´ėr ep´i lep´ti kəs\ mania following or replacing a grand mal seizure

fusion \fū´ zhən\ process of integrating separate images of the two eyes (of the same object) into a single impression

G **gait** \gāt\ manner of walking
galactemia \gə lak tē´mē ə\ galactosemia
galactose \gə lak´tōs\ a component of milk sugar or lactose
galactosemia \gə lak´´tō sē´mē ə\ hereditary defect in which galactose, produced from the sugar of milk, is not properly metabolized resulting in poor growth, mental defects, and death if untreated
galeophilia \gal´´ē ō fil´ē ə\ fondness for or pathological attraction to cats
galeophobia \gal´´ē ə fō´bē ə\ ailurophobia
galeropia \gal´´ə rōp´e ə\ unusual clarity of visual acuity; galeropsia
gall \gôl\ bile; skin irritation or sore
gall bladder \gôl blad´ėr\ the organ that stores bile, a substance used by the body to absorb and digest fats
galvanic skin response \gal van´ik skin rē spons\ (GSR) GSR measurement of skin electrical conductivity used to gauge emotional reaction to stimulation
gamete \gam´ēt\ reproductive cell of either male or female
gametocide \gə mē´ tə sīd\ agent that kills gametes
gametocyte \gə mē´tə sīt\ gamete produced cell
gametogenesis \gam´´ ə tō jeń´ ə sis\ production of gametes
gamin \gam´in\ a homeless boy; a street urchin
gamma globulin \gam´ə glōb´ū lin\ part of blood that contains the antibody activity
gamogenesis \gam´´ə jeń i sis\ reproduction through sexual means
gamomania \gam´´ə mā´nē ə\ abnormal preoccupation with becoming married
gamophobia \gam´´ə fō´bē ə\ unreasonable fear of marrying
gang \gang\ group of people tied together by common feelings or goals, with self-imposed discipline
ganglion \gang´glē ən\ (pl. ganglia) a nerve cell that serves as a control center outside the brain or spinal cord
Ganser's syndrome \gan´sėrz sin´drōm\ senseless behavior and speech characterized by foolish answers and acts
gargalesthesis \gär´´gə les thē´sis\ tickle feeling
gargoylism \gär´goil iz´´əm\ colloquial for Hurler's syndrome and other mucopolysaccharide disorders
garrulousness \gär´ə ləs nəs\ too much talk, often about unimportant things
gastric \gas´trik\ pertaining to the stomach
gastritis \gas trī´tis\ stomach inflammation characterized by pain or tenderness, nausea and vomiting
gastrodynia \gas´´trō din´ē ə\ stomach disorder, resulting in pain
gastrology \gas trol´ə jē\ study of the stomach
Gaucher's disease \gou´chėrz di´zēz\ familial disease of several forms that is characterized by accumulation of certain biochemical products producing a typical cell structure (Gaucher's cell), neurological deterioration, mental retardation and early death
gavage \gə väzh\ feeding directly into stomach by tube passed via nose or mouth
gender \jen´dėr\ sex
gene \jēn\ basic biologic unit of heredity which is located within the chromosome
genealogy \jēn´´ē al´ə jē\ record of ancestry
gene pool \jēn pūl\ sum of available genes within a given population
generalization \jen´´ėr ə li zā´shən\ in psychology, a response to a stimulus that is similar to the original stimulus
general practitioner \jen´ėr əl prak tish´ə nėr\ a physician who practices general medicine
generic \jə när´ik\ general, universal; referring to a kind, class or group
genesis \jen´i sis\ origin, beginning, way in which something is formed

49

genetic \jə net´ik\ pertaining to the genes or inheritance

genetic death \jə net´ik deth\ failure of an organism to reproduce and thereby not transmitting its genes to future generations

genetic drift \jə net´ik drift\ significant gene differences of an offshoot population from an original large population because the founders of the offshoot population were not representative of the larger population

genetic dyslexia \jə net´ik dis lek´sē ə\ syndrome of specific linguistic disabilities that restricts ability to learn to read, spell and write as well as expected

genetic engineering \jə net´ik en´´jə nēr´ing\ synthetic altering of the genes and their cell traits

genetics \jə net´iks\ the science that accounts for natural differences and resemblances among organisms related by descent; study of heredity and its variations

genic \jen´ik\ of or referring to genes

genital \jen´i təl\ pertaining to organs of reproduction

genitalia \jen´´i tā´lē ə\ organs of reproduction

genius \jēn´yəs\ outstanding ability, talent or characteristic; a person with outstanding talent

genoblast \jen´ə blast\ nucleus of the zygote

genocopy \jen´ə kop´´ē\ a characteristic produced by a gene that imitates the action of another gene

genome \jē´nōm\ chromosome set, the chromosomal complement of a gamete, or the corresponding complete set of genes

genophobia \jen´´ə fō´bē ə\ chronic, abnormal fear of sex

genotype \jen´ə tīp´´\ hereditary make-up of an individual

genus \jen´əs\ a class or group

geophagia \jē´´ō fa´jə\ the practice of eating dirt or clay

geriatrics \jăr´´ē a´triks\ medical branch that treats the elderly

germ \jėrm\ a microorganism; a bud or seed

German measles \jėr´mən mē´zelz\ rubella

germicide \jėr´mi sīd\ something that kills germs

germ plasm \jėrm plaz´əm\ reproductive cells

gerontology \jăr´´ən tol´ə jē\ science of old age

gerontophobia \jə ron´´tə fō´bē ə\ abnormal fear of old age

Gerstmann's syndrome \gėrst´məns sin´drōm\ neurological disorder characterized by finger agnosia, lateral confusion, agraphia and acalculia

gestalt \gəsh tält´\ any unified whole whose properties are different from its parts in summation

gestation \je stā´shən\ period of pregnancy

gesticulate \je stik´yə lāt´´\ use gestures to express emotions

gibberish \jib´ėr ish\ incoherent speech; immature pattern of speaking that omits final and difficult sounds

gibbosity \gi bos´i tē\ condition of having a hunchback

gibbous \gib´əs\ humped or hump-backed

giddy \gid´ē\ dizzy

gifted \gif´təd\ having a high level of intelligence, achievement and/or talent

gigantism \jī gan´tiz əm\ abnormally large body development due to pituitary malfunction

gimp \gimp\ slang for limp

glabrous \gla´brəs\ smooth or hairless

glaucoma \glau kō´mə\ increased pressure within the eye due to accumulation of aqueous humor causing visual impairment

glioma \glī ō mə\ type of brain tumor

gliosis \glī ō´sis\ abnormal growth of fibrous tissue in the brain or spinal cord

glossal \glos´əl\ referring to the tongue

glossectomy \glo sek´tə mē\ surgical removal of part or all of the tongue

glossitis \glo sī´tis\ inflammation of the tongue

glossograph \glō´sə graf\ instrument for recording movement of the tongue during speech

glossolalia \glos´´ə lā´lē ə\ speech that has meaning to originator but not to listener

glossopharyngeal \glos´´ō fə rin´jē əl\ pertaining to the pharynx and tongue

glossophobia \glos´´ə fō´bē ə\ extreme fear of talking, usually related to anticipation of articulation error; laliophobia

glossoplegia \glos´´ ə plē´jē ə\ paralysis of the tongue

glossotomy \glos ot´ə mē\ incising of the tongue

glottal vibration \glot´əl vī brā´shən\ opening and closing of space between the vocal cords

glottis \glot´is\ the opening between the vocal cords

glucose \glū´kōs\ type of sugar; dextrose

gluteus \glü´tē əs\ any of several buttock muscles

gluttony \glut´ə nē\ excessive eating and drinking

glycemia \glī sē´mē ə\ presence of sugar, specifically glucose in the blood

glycogen \gli´kə jən\ carbohydrate substance found abundantly in liver; also called animal starch

glycogenoses \glī´´kə je nō´səs\ a group of glycogen metabolism disorders characterized by cardiac and liver abnormalities, progressive muscular weakness and possible mental retardation; there is early demise in some types

gnosia \nō´zhə\ faculty of perceiving, recognizing and understanding

goiter \goi´tėr\ pathological enlargement of the thyroid gland

gonad \gō´nad\ ovary or testicle; the male or female sex gland

gonioscope \go´nē ə skōp´´\ magnifying instrument used to examine the anterior portion of the eye

gonococcus \gon´´ə kok´əs\ infectious microorganism that causes gonorrhea

gonorrhea \gon´´ə rē´ə\ venereal disease capable of crippling and causing sterility; the disease may be transmitted from mother to child at the time of birth

grade school \grād skül\ an elementary school set up or graded according to pupil progress

grammar \gram´ėr\ the system or the study of the system that underlies a language

grandiosity \gran´´dē os´i tē\ abnormal overestimation of self; pompous; grand in an imposing way

grand mal epilepsy \grand mäl ep´ə lep´´sē\ generalized tonic-clinic convulsions accompanied by loss of consciousness; convulsions may or may not be preceded by an aura

grapheme \graf´ēm\ written symbol that represents a sound in oral language

graphesthesia \graf´´əs thē´zhə\ ability to identify letters of the alphabet or numbers when traced on the skin

graphic language \graf´ik lan´gwidj\ symbols used to transmit or record ideas, concepts, events, etc.

graphomania \graf´´ə mā´nē ə\ compulsion to write

graphomotor \graf´ə mō´´tėr\ involving the muscle movements that occur in writing

graphorrhea \grə fŏr´ē ə\ profuse, meaningless writing often associated with graphomania

gratification \grat´´ə fə kā´shən\ state of having a desire satisfied

gravid \grav´id\ pregnant

gray matter \grā mat´ėr\ nerve cells of the brain and spinal cord; informal, the brain or thought organ

Greig's disease \grāgs di zēz´\ hypertelorism

grimace \grim´əs\ facial expression that is distorted, expressing pain, fear or other strong negative emotion

gristle \gris´əl\ cartilage

grooming \grüm´ing\ the care of one's person and dress

gross motor coordination \grōs mō´tĕr cō ôr´´di nā´shən\ the harmonious functioning of the major large body muscles

gross motor development \grōs mō´tĕr di vel´əp mənt\ maturation of large muscle activity

group dynamics \grüp dī nam´iks\ interaction of assemblage of persons

group intelligence test \grüp in tel´ə gens test\ test measurement of many at one time

group process \grüp pro´ses\ the way a group approaches problem solving

group therapy \grüp thăr´ə pē\ psychological treatment in which a number of patients interact for their mutual benefit under the guidance of a professional

growing pains \grō´ing pānz\ neuralgic or psychological pains due to developmental stresses

growth \grōth\ increase in size or ability; progress toward a state of increased maturation

growth principle \grōth prin´si pəl\ in Rogerian psychology, the idea that self-actualizing forces direct a person toward greater mental health and adjustment

guidance \gīd´əns\ assistance offered to help one cope with problems

guide dog \gīd dog\ dog trained to assist the blind with mobility; seeing eye dog

guilt \gilt\ feelings of regret for having violated one's own ethical or moral principles

guilt feelings \gilt fēl´ings\ feeling of having done something wrong

gustatory \gus´tə tôr´´ē\ refers to the sense of taste

gutteral \gut´ėr əl\ raspy, throaty, low-pitched voice quality; referring speech to sounds articulated in the back of the mouth

gynecology \gī´´nə kol´ə jē\ the branch of medicine concerned with disorders of the female reproductive system

gynecomastia \gī´´nə kō mas´tē ə\ abnormal breast development in a male

gynephobia \gī´´nə fō´bē ə\ chronic, unreasonable fear of women

gyrus \jī´rəs\ convolution of cerebral hemisphere surface

H **habilitation** \hə bil´´i tā´shən\ training process to improve the total functioning of a person

habit \hab´it\ fixed behavior established by repetition

habitat \hab´i tat´´\ surroundings, living area

habit spasm \hab´it spaz´əm\ meaningless, ticlike, recurring contraction of muscle or muscles, essentially a mannerism rather than true tic

habituation \hə bich´´ū ā´shən\ adaptation to the environment; habit formation

habromania \hab´´rə mā´´nē ə\ mental illness marked by inappropriate gaiety and cheerfulness; amenomania

hadephobia \hā´´də fō´bē ə\ morbid, unremitting fear of hell

hagiotherapy \hā´´jē ō thăr´ə pē\ miraculous healing through divine intervention

halation \hā lā´shən\ blurring of the visual image due to strong light source behind the object being viewed

half-life \haf līf\ the time it takes to reduce the radioactivity of a particular element to one-half its original level through radioactive decay

halfway house \haf´wā hous\ facility designed to provide transition from residential institutional facility to the community

halitosis \hal´´i tō´sis\ offensive or bad breath

hallucination \hə lü´´sə nā´shən\ experience of sensation in absence of appropriate external stimulation; may be auditory, visual, olfactory, gustatory or tactile

hallucinogen \hə lü´sə nə jen´´\ drug or chemical agent that will produce hallucinations

hallucinogenic agents \hə lü´´sə nō jen´ik ā´jents\ mind-expanding drugs, such as LSD, mescaline, marijuana and others

halo effect \hā´lō ə fekt´\ the tendency when rating one attribute of an individual to be influenced by one or more attributes that are not relevant to the rating

hamartophobia \ha´´mär tə fō´bē ə\ extreme, persistent fear of error or sinning

hamartoplasia \ha´´mär tə plā´zhə\ overdevelopment of tissue during a healing process

hammer \ham´ér\ the small, hammer-shaped bone of the middle ear; the malleus

handedness \han´dəd nəs\ distinguisable preference to usage of one hand more than the other as in writing, throwing and eating

handicap \han´dē kap´´\ condition that constitutes a competitive disadvantage for its possessor

handicapism \han´dē kap iz´´əm\ stereotype or bias toward a handicap or a handicapped person

handicapped person \han´dē kapt´´ pér´sən\ individual who is impaired physically, intellectually or emotionally to such an extent that his or her limitations often interfere with adapting to societal expectations

haphalgesia \haf´´əl jē´zhə\ pain sensation produced by minor tactile stimulation

haphephobia \haf´´ə fō´bē ə\ unreasonable fear of being touched

haploid \hap´loid\ having a single set of chromosomes as in gametes

haplology \hap lol´ə jē\ syllable omission due to rapid speaking

haptic \hap´tik\ sense of touch

hard drugs \härd drugz\ narcotics, such as heroin, that are injected into the vein

hard of hearing \härd uv hēr´ing\ impaired hearing with enough residual for practical use

hard palate \härd pal´ət\ bony anterior part of roof of mouth

harelip \hăr´lip\ cleavage of the upper lip that is usually due to congenital closure failure of maxillary processes

Hartnup disease \härt´nəp di zēz´\ hereditary amino acid transport disorder characterized by a variety of central nervous system abnormalities

hashish \hash´ish\ drug made from leaves and stalks of Indian hemp that may be chewed or smoked

hawthorne effect \hä´thôrn ə fekt´\ altered performance by a subject due to awareness of his/her participation in a study

headache \hed´āk\ pain that may occur in various portions of the head, may be acute or chronic

hearing acuity \hēr´ing a kū´i tē\ degree of ability to detect the presence of sound through the sensory apparatus of the ear

hearing aid \hēr´ing ād\ device used to amplify or focus sound waves in the ear

hearing handicap \hēr´ing han´dē kap´\ partial loss of auditory function

hearing loss \hēr´ing los\ detectable reduction in auditory acuity; levels are—mild, 15 to 25 decibels; moderate, 25 to 55 decibels; marked, 55 to 75 decibels; profound, 75 decibels or more

hebephrenia \hē´´bə frē´nē ə\ type of schizophrenia characterized by bizarre inappropriate behavior and shallowness of affect

hebetic \hi bet´ik\ referring to the time of puberty

hebetude \heb´ə tüd\ lethargy; emotional dullness

hedonia \hē dō´nē ə\ abnormal cheerfulness

hedonism \hē´dən iz´´əm\ philosophy that considers the attainment of happiness as the highest good; devotion to pleasure

hedonophobia \hē´´dan ə fō´bē ə\ fear of pleasure or activities that promote pleasure

heliophobia \hē´´lē ə fō´bē ə\ abnormal fear of sunlight

heliotherapy \hē´´lē ō thär´ə pē\ sun bathing for therapeutic purposes

helix \hē´liks\ the upper edge of the external ear

Heller's disease \hel´ērz di zēz´\ dementia infantalis, degenerative metabolic disorder characterized by brain atrophy and nerve cell degeneration; occurs among young children

helminthophobia \hel´minth ə fō´bē ə\ extreme fear of infestation by worms

hemanalysis \hē´´mə nal´i sis\ examination of the blood for disease or other abnormality

hemangioma \hē´´man jē ō´mə\ a benign tumor of the blood vessels

hematology \hē´´mə tol´ə jē\ science of the morphology, function and diseases of the blood

hematoma \hē´´mə tō´mə\ tumor that contains effused blood

hematophobia \hē´´mə tə fō´bē ə\ hemophobia

hematazoon \hē´mə tə zō´ən\ any microorganism that dwells in blood

hemianencephaly \hem´´ē ən en sef´ə lē\ congential cranial abnormality characterized by absence of one side of the brain

hemianopia \hem´´ē ə nō´ pē ə\ blindness or reduced vision in one-half of the visual field

hemianopsia \hem´´ē ə nōp´ sē ə\ blindness in one-half of the visual field of one or both eyes; hemiopia

hemiapraxia \hem´´ē ə prak´sē ə\ loss of coordination on one side of the body

hemiatrophy \hem´´ē a´trə fē\ wasting away of one side of a body or a body part

hemicrania \hem´´ē krā´nē ə\ severe, recurring headaches affecting one side of the head

hemiopia \hem´´ē ō´pē ə\ hemianopia

hemiparesis \hem´´ē pə rē´sis\ weakness of one lateral half of the body

hemiplegia \hem´´i plē´jē ə\ paralysis in which one side of the body is involved

hemiscotosis \hem´´ē skə tō´sis\ hemianopsia

hemisphere \hem´i sfēr´\ either lateral half of the brain

hemizygous \hem´ē zi´gəs\ having only one of a pair of genes that determines a particular trait

hemoglobin \hē´mə glō´´bin\ oxygen-carrying molecules of the blood

hemopathy \hē mop´ə thē\ disease or abnormal condition of the blood

hemophilia \hē´´mə fēl´ē ə\ blood disease characterized by reduced ability to coagulate; forms A and B transmitted as sex-linked recessives; form C due to an autosomal dominant gene mechanism

hemophiliac \hē´´mə fēl´ē ak\ person afflicted with hemophilia

hemophobia \hē´´mə fō´bē ə\ abnormal fear of blood

hemorrhage \hem´ėr ij\ discharge of blood from the vessels

hepatic \hi pat´ik\ referring to the liver

hepatitis \hep´´ə tī´tis\ inflammation of the liver

hepatolenticular degeneration \hep´´ə tō len tik´ū lėr dē´´jén ėr ā´shən\ Wilson's disease

hepatomegaly \hep´´ə tō meg´ə lē\ condition of increased size of the liver

hepatosplenomegaly \hep´´ə tō´´splē nō māg´ə lē\ condition of increased size of liver and spleen

herbicide \hėr´bi sīd´´\ chemical used to kill plants

hereditary \hə red´i tär´´ē\ refers to passing of traits, characteristics or conditions from parents to offspring

hereditary spinocerebellar ataxia \hə red´i tär´´ē spī´´nō sär ə bel´ėr ə tak´sē ə\ Friedreich's ataxia

heredity \hə red´i tē\ genetic transmission of inherited traits from one generation to the next

heredofamilial \hə red´´ō fə mil´ē əl\ referring to hereditary traits confined to certain families

heredoimmunity \hə red´ō i mūn´i tē\ inherited immunity

heredopathia \hə red´´ō path´ē ə\ inherited defect

heredosyphilis \hē red´´ō sif´ə lis\ congenital syphilis

heritable \hăr´i tə bəl\ possessing the capability of being inherited; inheritable

heritage \hăr´i tij\ that which is passed down from generation to generation

hermaphroditism \hėr mof´rə dī tiz´´əm\ condition in which both male and female genital structures occur in an individual; hermaphrodism

hernia \hėr´nē ə\ protrusion of tissue or part of an organ through an unnatural opening

heroin \hăr´ō in\ habit-forming morphine derivative that is widely used illegally

herpes facialis \hėr´pēz fā´´shē a´lis\ vesicular facial eruption, often around the lips (herpes labialis) that are commonly called cold sores

herpes simplex \hėr´pez sim´pleks\ incurable, infectious disease caused by herpes viruses I and II; either form may be venereal and under certain circumstances may be transmitted prenatally or during the birth process to offspring

herpes virus \hėr´ pēz vī´rəs\ the viral agents that cause various types of herpetic infections

heterocentric \het´´ėr ō sen´trik\ directed outward, towards others; opposite of egocentric

heterochromosome \het´´ėr ə krŏ´mə sōm\ sex chromosome

heterogametic \het´´ėr ə gam´ēt ik\ producing differing kinds of gametes, such as X and Y

heterogeneous \het´ėr ə jē´nē əs\ composed of differing or variable parts or elements

heterometropia \het´´ėr ə mə trō´pē ə\ condition in which differing types of refraction exist between eyes, as when one eye is myopic and the other is hyperopic

heterophasia \het´´ə rō fā´zhə\ uttering words other than intended

heterophonia \het´´ə rō fō´nē ə\ abnormality of voice quality

heterophoria \het´´ėr ə fôr´ē ə\ tendency of the eyes to deviate from parallel axes when fusion is disrupted

heterophthalmia \het´´ə rôf thal´mē ə\ marked difference between two eyes in axes direction, size or color

heterophthongia \het´´ə röf thon´jē ə\ any abnormality of speech

heteroploidy \het´´ér ə ploi´dē\ state of having an abnormal number of chromosomes for a species

heteroptics \het´´ə rop´tiks\ visual hallucinations

heterosexual \het´ér ə sek´shü əl\ referring to the opposite sex

heterosexuality \het´´ér ə sek´´shü al´i tē\ attraction to or love for the opposite sex

heterotaxis \het´´ér ə tak´sis\ abnormal arrangement or positioning of body parts

heterotopia \het´´ér ə tō´pē ə\ abnormal placement of organs or other tissue

heterotropia \het´´ér ə trō´pē ə\ strabismus; cross-eyed status

heterotypic \het´´ér ə tip´ik\ referring to the meiotic divisional stage

heterozygous \het´´ér ə zī´gəs\ possessing differing genes with regard to a particular trait or condition

heuristic \hū ris´tik\ stimulating investigation, research or learning

hidrosis \hī drō´sis\ excessive sweating

hierarchy \hi´ər är´´kē\ arrangement in rank order, as in a hierarchy of needs

hieromania \hī´´ə rō mā´nē ə\ morbid preoccupation with religion; religious frenzy

hierophobia \hī´´ə rō fō´bē ə\ chronic, unreasonable fear of religious objects

hippus \hip´əs\ condition in which the pupils of the eye contract and dilate rhythmically and independently of changes in light intensity

hirsute \hér´sūt\ hairy

hirsutism \hér´´sū tiz´əm\ excessive amount of hair

histidinemia \his´´ti di nē´mē ə\ deficiency of enzyme histidase resulting in an abnormal level of histidine in blood; findings of impaired speech, occasional growth retardation and mental retardation have been mentioned; transmitted as an autosomal recessive

histogram \his´tə gram\ graph of a frequency distribution

histology \hi stol´ə jē\ study of tissues

historical approach \hi stôr´i kəl ə prōch\ a counseling technique aimed at solving problems by recounting past events that led to the problem

hoarseness \hôrs´nəs\ cough; low pitch voice sound

Hodgkin's disease \hoj´kinz di zēz\ pseudoleukemia

holism \hō´liz əm\ theory that the qualities of a living organism are derived from its wholeness rather than from the sum of constituent parts

homeostasis \hō´´mē ə stā´sis\ process of maintaining equilibrium

homeotypic \hō´´mē ə tip´ik\ referring to the second meiotic divisional stage

homicidomania \hō´mə sīd´´ə mā´nē ə\ compulsive, morbid desire to kill another human

homoeroticism \hō´´mō ə rot´i siz əm\ sexual interest in individuals of the same sex; a more general term than homosexuality

homogeneity \hō´´mə jə nē i tē\ quality of being homogenous

homogeneous \hō´´mə jē´nē əs\ composed of similar parts or elements

homophemes \hō´mə fēms\ differing sounds that appear the same on the lips when observed by a lip-reader

homophonic \hom´´ə fon´ik\ referring to the same sound

homosexual \hō´´mə sek´shü əl\ referring to the same sex; a person who prefers sexual activity with members of the same sex

homosexuality \hō´´mə sek´´shü al´i tē\ directing sexual desire toward the same sex

homotaxis \hō´´mə tak´sis\ having the same arrangement of body parts

homozygote \hō´mə zī´gōt\ an organism that has received like genes from each parent with regard to a particular characteristic

homozygous \hō´´mə zī´gəs\ possessing

identical genes with regard to a particular trait condition

Hoover cane \hü´vėr kān\ a long, slender white cane used by the blind for motility assistance

hormone \hôr´mōn\ biochemical substance produced by the body that has particular effect on the functioning of certain organs

hospitalism \hos´´pit əl iz´əm\ neurotic desire to be hospitalized

hostility \ho stil´i tē\ aggression directed toward a source of anger or frustration

Huffer's neuropathy \huf´ėrz nėr op´ə thē\ central nervous system disorder caused by inhalation of hallucinogenic chemicals

human engineering \hu´mən en´´jə nėr´ing\ study of relationships between equipment and design and the physical, sensory and emotional capabilities of man with special regard for work efficiency and safety

humanism \hū´mə niz´´əm\ philosophy that human needs, interests, values and welfare should predominate

humerus \hū´mėr əs\ bone of the arm between shoulder and elbow

humpback \hump´bak\ hunchback

hunchback \hunch´bak\ kyphosis; a person with kyphosis

Hunter's syndrome \hun´tėrz sin´drōm\ mucopolysaccharidosis II; X-linked recessive gene defect that results in a number of developmental anomalies, mental retardation and early demise

Huntington's chorea \ hun´ting tunz kôr ē´ə\ hereditary, progressive neurological disorder characterized by ataxia, chorea and mental disturbances

Hurler's syndrome \hėr´lerz sin´drōm\ mucopolysaccharidosis I; hereditary defect of polysaccharide metabolism that results in a number of developmental abnormalities, mental retardation and early death; also called gargoylism

Hutchinson's teeth \huch´in sunz tēth\ notched or peg teeth, a characteristic of congenital syphilis

hyaline membrane disease \hī´ə lin mem´brān di zēz´\ a lung disorder of premature infants that interferes with the oxygenation process

hybrid \hī´brid\ progeny of parents of differing species

hydranencephaly \hī´´dren en sef´ə lē\ partial or complete absence of cerebral hemisphere with cerebrospinal fluid replacing the missing brain tissue

hydrencephalocele \hī´dren sef´ə lō sēl\ cranial defect wherein brain tissue and cerebrospinal fluid herniate through the skull

hydrencephalomeningocele \hī´´dren sef´´ə lō mə nin´gə sēl\ cranial defect in which brain tissue and cerebrospinal fluid herniate through the meninges, forming a bump or protuberance

hydrencephalus \hī´´dren sef´ə ləs\ hydrocephalus

hydrocephalus \hī´´drə sef´ə ləs\ cranial abnormality characterized by an imbalance or stoppage in the flow of the cerebrospinal fluid; as the fluid accumulates, the head may enlarge, and mental retardation and a wide variety of sensory and motor defects may result

hydrodipsomania \hī´´drə dip´´sə mā´nē ə\ extreme thirst related to epileptic attack

hydromicrocephaly \hi´´drə mī´krə sef´ə lē\ form of microcephaly characterized by an abnormal accumulation of cerebrospinal fluid

hydrophobia \hī´drə fō´bē ə\ rabies; also abnormal fear of water

hydrophthalmos \hī´´drəf thal´məs\ congenital glaucoma characterized by an abnormally large eye present at birth or in early infancy

hydrotherapy \hi´´drə thăr´ə pē\ use of water in the treatment of disease

hygiene \hī´jēn\ the study of health and its maintenance

hygieology \hī´´jē ol´ə jē\ science of sanitation and good health practices

hypacusia \hip´´ə kū´zhə\ difficulty in hearing

hypalgesia \hip´´əl jē´zhə\ reduced pain sensitivity

hypengyophobia \hī pen´´jē ə fō´bē ə\ chronic, unreasonable fear of responsibility

hyperactivity \hī´´pėr ak tiv´ i tē\ excessive movement

hyperacusia \hī´´pėr ə kū´zhə\ painful sensitivity to noise or sound; hyperacusis

hyperalgesia \hī´pėr al jē´zhə\ increased sensitivity to painful stimulation

hyperbilirubinemia \hī´´pėr bil´´i rü´bi nē´mē ə\ abnormally high levels of bilirubin in the blood

hypercalcemia \hī´´pėr kal sē´mē ə\ excess of calcium in the blood

hyperdactylia \hī´´pėr dak til´ē ə\ more than the normal number of fingers or toes

hyperdistractibility \hī´´pėr dis trakt´´ti bil´i tē\ rapid attention shift from stimulus to stimulus without recognition of relevant stimulation

hyperesthesia \hī´´pėr es thē´zhə\ abnormally high sensitivity to pain, temperature or sense of touch

hyperflexion \hī´´pėr flek´shən\ forced overbending of an arm, leg or other body part

hyperfunction \hī´´pėr funk´shən\ vocal production that is strained; excessive activity of an organ

hypergenesis \hī´´pėr jen´ə sis\ overdevelopment of an organ or body part; hypertrophy

hyperglycemia \hī´´pėr glī sē´mē ə\ condition characterized by abnormally high level of glucose in the blood

hypergnosia \hī´´pėr nō´zhə\ a condition characterized by distortion of reality and projection of inner conflicts upon the environment

hyperkinesia \hī´´pėr ki nē´ zhə\ abnormally high level of motor activity

hyperkinetic \hī´´pėr ki net´ik\ describes excessive movement

hyperlexia \hī´´pėr lek´sē ə\ sight-reading words without comprehension

hypermania \hī´´pėr mā´nē ə\ a condition marked by disorientation, hyperactivity and excessive emotionality

hypermegasoma \hī´´pėr meg´ə sō´´mə\ gigantism

hypermetropia \hī´´pėr mi trō´pē ə\ hyperopia

hypermnesia \hī´´pėrm nē´zhə\ facility of memory

hypermotility \hi´´pėr mō til´i tē\ more than normal flexion of the joints

hypernasality \hī´´pėr nā sal´i tē\ excessive nasal resonance in voice quality

hyperopia \hī´´pėr ō´pē ə\ farsightedness; refractive error in which the point of focus of an eye at rest falls behind the retina

hyperorexia \hī´´pėr ə rek´sē ə\ abnormal craving for food

hyperostosis \hī´´pėr o stō´sis\ bony overgrowth

hyperparathyroidism \hī´´pėr păr ə thī´roi diz´´ əm\ over-activity of the parathyroid gland with softening of the bones, spontaneous fractures, weakness and pain

hyperphagia \hī´´pėr fā´jē ə\ excessive craving for food; bulimia

hyperphoria \hī´´pėr fôr´ē ə\ type of heterophoria in which the line of sight deviates upward when fusion is disrupted

hyperphasia \hī´´pėr fā´zhə\ garrulousness

hyperphrenia \hī´´pėr frē´ nē ə\ state of excessive amount of mental activity

hyperpituitarism \hī´´pėr pi tü´i tə riz´´əm\ a state in which there is overactivity of the pituitary gland

hyperplasia \hī´´pėr plā´zhē ə\ abnormal increase in number of cells in a body part

hyperpnea \hī pėrp´nē ə\ heavy breathing

hyperprosexia \hī´´pėr prō sek´sē ə\ the inability to ignore a stimulus

hyperpyrexia \hī´´pėr pī rek´sē ə\ extremely high fever

hypersomnia \hi´´pėr som´nē ə\ extreme sleepiness in the absence of fatigue or sleep deprivation

hypertelorism \hi´´pėr tel´ėr iz´´əm\ ocular hypertelorism refers to a condition in which the eyes are unusually wide spaced; may be associated with craniofacial abnormalities and mental retardation

hypertension \hi´´pėr ten´shən\ elevated blood pressure

hyperthermia \hi´´pėr thėr´mē ə\ abnormally high temperature

hyperthymia \hi´´pėr thī´mē ə\ state of increased emotionality

hyperthyroidism \hi´´pėr thī´roid iz´´əm\ excessive action of the thyroid gland that may result in exophthalmos and hyperactivity

hypertonia \hi´´pėr tō´nē ə\ increased muscle tone

hypertrophy \hi pėr´trə fē\ abnormal overgrowth of a body part due to increase in size of individual cells

hypertropia \hi´´pėr trō´pē ə\ a type of strabismus in which one eye remains fixed upon an object while the other rolls upward

hyperuricemia \hi´´pėr yūr´´i sē´mē ə\ Lesch-Nyhan syndrome; abnormal release of uric acid in urine

hyperventilation \hi´´pėr ven´´tə lā´shən\ rapid, deep breathing that may precipitate a seizure in certain forms of epilepsy

hypnosis \hip nō´sis\ induced state similar to sleep, involving an increased susceptibility to suggestion

hypnotherapy \hip´´nō thăr´ə pē\ treatment using hypnotism

hypoactivity \hi´´pō ak tiv´i tē\ abnormally low level of physical activity

hypoacusis \hi´pō ə kū´sis\ hearing impairment

hypocenter \hi´´pō seń tėr\ exact center of a nuclear explosion

hypochondria \hi´´pə kon´drē ə\ unnecessary and excessive preoccupation with one's health

hypofunction \hi´´pō funk´shən\ low or inadequate functioning

hypogeusesthesia \hi´´pə jūs´´ es thē´ zhə\ impairment in the sense of taste

hypoglycemia \hi´´pō glī sē´mē ə\ abnormally low blood glucose level

hypognathous \hi pog´nəth əs\ enlarged and protruding mandible

hypokinesia \hi´´pō ki nē´zhə\ abnormally low level of motor activity

hypologia \hi´´pə lō´jē ə\ decreased speech due to mental defect

hypomania \hi´´pə mā´´nē ə\ mild state of madness

hypomnesia \hi´´pom nē´zhə\ deficient memory; absent-mindedness

hypomotility \hi´´pō mō til´i tē\ reduced movement or flexibility, as in the joints

hypomyotonia \hi´´pə mī´´ə tō´nē ə\ abnormally decreased muscle tone

hyponasality \hi´´pō nā sal´i tē\ lack of normal nasality in voice

hypophobia \hi´´pō fō´bē ə\ lack of normal fear

hypophonia \hi´´pō fō´nē ə\ abnormal weakness of the voice due to speech muscle incoordination

hypophoria \hi´´pō fôr´ē ə\ downward deviation of the visual axis of one eye as compared to the other eye

hypophrenia \hi´´pō frē´nē ə\ term used as a synonym of mental retardation

hypopituitarism \hi´´pō pi tü´´i tə riz´əm\ a condition of underactivity of the pituitary gland that may result in obesity, sterility and dwarfism

hypoplasia \hi´´pə plā´´zhə\ underdevelopment of an organ or cell structure

hypopraxia \hi´´pə prak´sē ə\ listlessness or reduced activity

hypoprosexia \hi´´pō prō sek´sē ə\ abnormal shortness of attention span

hyposmia \hi poz´mē ə\ impairment in the sense of smell

hyposthenia \hi´´pos thē´nē ə\ weakness, lack of strength and vigor

hypotelorism \hi´´pō tel´ėr iz əm\ abnormally decreased distance between two organs, expecially the eyes

hypotension \hi´´pə ten´shən\ condi-

tion characterized by abnormally
decreased blood pressure

hypothermia \hī′′ pə thėr′
mē ə\ significantly subaverage body
temperature

hypothesis \hī poth′i sis\ proposition
set forth to explain observed phenomena

hypothyroidism \hī′′pō thī′roid
iz′′əm\ cretinism; deficiency in thyroid activity that may result in mental
defects and physical abnormalities

hypotonia \hī′′pō to′nē ə\ flabbiness or
loss of tonicity of muscles

hypotonicity \hī′′pə tō nis′i tē\ reduced
muscle tone

hypotropia \hī′′pə trō′pē ə\ eye defect
in which one eye turns downward
with respect to the other eye

hypoxemia \hī′′pok sē′mē ə\ state of
insufficient oxygen in the blood

hypoxia \hī pok′sē ə\ condition characterized by insufficiency of available
oxygen

hypsicephaly \hip′si sėf′ə lē\ acrocephaly

hysteria \hi stēr′ē ə\ neurosis with
changes in sensory or motor function; violent emotional outbursts
may also occur

I **ianthinopsia** \ī´´an thi nop´shə\ a condition in which vision is violet tinged

iatrogenic \ī a´´trə jen´ik\ of medical origin; especially refers to symptoms or conditions caused by medical treatment

ictal \ik´təl\ referring to a stroke or epileptic attack

icterus \ik´tér əs\ jaundice

id \id\ part of the personality concerned with instinctual drives

ideation \ī´´dē ā´shən\ the process of conceiving ideas

identification \ī´den ti fi kā´ shən\ psychological process in which a person associates himself with other persons, groups or organizations, as a means of gaining security, self-esteem

idiocy \id´ē ə sē\ profound mental retardation

idioglossia \id´´ē ə glos´ē ə\ idiolalia; invented language resulting from omission, substitution, distortion, and transposition of speech sounds, often spoken by twins

idiogram \id´ē ə gram´\ diagrammatic illustration of chromosomes, more commonly called karyotype

idiolalia \id´´ē ə lā´lē ə\ mental disturbance characterized by the use of an invented language

idiopathic \id´´ē ə path´ik\ of unknown origin

idiopathy \id´´ē op´ə thē\ primary disease of spontaneous origin

idiosyncrasy \id´´ē ə sing´krə sē\ characteristic or trait peculiar to an individual

idiot \id´ē ət\ term historically used to refer to a profoundly retarded person

idiotropic \id´´ē ə trop´ik\ introspective, characterizing a person who prefers to turn inward for satisfaction rather than toward others

idiot savant \id´ē ət sə vänt´\ a person possessing a great talent or proficiency in one area while otherwise functioning as mentally retarded

illiteracy \i lit´ér ə sē\ inability to read or write as a result of lack of education

illusion \i lü´zhən\ misinterpretation of data received through senses

imbecile \im´bi sil\ term historically used to refer to persons classified in the severe and low moderate ranges of mental retardation

immobilization \im mō´´bil i zā´shən\ action resulting in rendering a person unable to continue an activity that has been corrected or adversely criticized; action resulting in rendering a body part immovable as in the use of a cast in orthopedics

immoralism \i môr´ə liz´´əm\ opposition or refusal to accept the prevailing ethics and morals of one's society

immunogenetics \i mū´´nō jə net´iks\ that branch of genetics that studies heritable immunity

immunology \im´´yə nol´ə jē\ medical branch that deals with immunity

imperception \im´´pér sep´shən\ inability to interpret sensory information correctly

impotence \im´pə təns\ inability to control one's destiny or reach desired goals; specifically refers to inability of the male to perform normal sexual act

impregnate \im preg´nāt\ to fertilize or make pregnant

imprinting \im prin´ting\ a special learning process that takes place very early in life

improbity \im prō´bi tē\ immorality; wickedness; lack of ethical principles

impulse \im´puls\ sudden desire toward action without delay or reflection

impulsivity \im´´pul siv´i tē\ impulsiveness; tendency to act quickly without anticipating consequences

impunitive \im pū´ni tiv\ tendency toward conciliation in conflicts between self and others

impunity \im pū´ni tē\ freedom from punishment or penalty

inadequacy \in ad´ə kwə sē\ insufficiency; incompetence

inanition \in´´ə ni´shən\ body deterioration due to malnutrition

inarticulate \in´´är tik´ū lət\ not adjacent or joined; unclear speech

inborn \in´bôrn\ inherited; innate

inbreeding \in´brē ding\ mating of related individuals; consanguineous conception

incapacious \in´´kə pā´shəs\ mentally limited; mentally incapable of a task

incest \in´cest\ socially disapproved sexual activity between persons closely related by common ancestry

incidence \in´si dəns\ rate at which a disease or condition occurs

incoherence \in´´kō hēr´əns\ disconnected and unrelated thoughts or utterances

incompetent \in kom´pə tənt\ state (legal) of being unable to manage one's own affairs adequately due to physical or mental subnormality

incontinent \in kon´tə nənt\ failure to establish or maintain toilet control at appropiate age levels

incubator \ing´kyə bā´´tèr\ chamber used to maintain appropriate temperature, humidity and oxygen levels for babies requiring intensive care; isolette

incus \ing´kəs\ middle bone of the three bones in the middle ear

indagate \in´də gāt´´\ to research or investigate

indigence \in´di jəns\ poverty

indigenous \in dij ´ə nəs\ native to a particular region; originating in a particular area

individual intelligence test \in´´di vid´ jū əl in tel´i jens test\ evaluative instrument administered to one person at a time, such as the Stanford-Binet and the Wechsler tests for adults and children

ineducable \in ej´ū kə bəl\ incapable of profiting from academic instruction due to mental or emotional disorders

infant \in´fant\ child during the first year of life

infantile \in´fən tīl\ refers to characteristics or traits of infants

infantile autism \in´fən til´ ä´tiz əm\ autism; infantile; condition characterized by severe withdrawal and inappropriate response to external stimulation

infantile paralysis \in´fən til´´ pə ral´i sis\ poliomyelitis

infantilism \in´fan ti liz´´əm\ the presence of childish behavior or physical characteristics in an adult; childlike speech patterns in an adult

infantilization \in fan´´ti lī zā´ shən\ treatment of adults and adolescents that restricts their freedom and decision making as though they were young children

infecund \in fē´kənd\ infertile

inferiority complex \in fēr´´ē ôr´ i tē kom´pleks\ feelings of inadequacy and incompetence

infertility \in´´fèr til´i tē\ condition of being incapable of reproduction

inflection \in flek´shən\ change pitch and loudness of speech to vary meaning of words

infrahuman \in´´frə hū´mən\ human behavior or characteristics resembling or in common with lower animals; pertaining to animals other than man

ingestion \in jes´chən\ the act of taking food or other substances into the body by eating

inherent \in hăr´ənt\ intrinsic; provided by nature

inheritance \in hăr´i təns\ the process of receiving traits or characteristics from one's parents through genetic action

inhibition \in´´i bish´ən\ restraint of impulse behavior

innate \i nāt´\ present in individual since conception

inner speech \in´ner spēch\ mental image of words in terms of auditory, visual or kinesthetic sensations

innervation \in´ér vā´shən\ the activation of a body part by a nerve

insalubrious \in´´sə lū´brē əs\ unhealthful

insanity \in san´i tē\ social or legal term for mental illness

insecurity \in''sə kūr´i tē\ feeling of anxiety that may be unwarranted

insemination \in sem''i nā´shən\ deposition of seminal fluid within the vagina

insenescence \in''sə nes´əns\ the aging process

insight \in´sīt\ the perception with understanding of the inner nature of a concept, situation, event or behavior

insomnia \in som´nē ə\ chronic inability to sleep

inspiration \in''spi rā´shən\ taking air into the lungs

instinct \in´stinkt\ inherited tendency to react to certain environmental conditions and stimuli in a particular way

instinctual \in stink´shū əl\ refers to behavior activated by genetic programming rather than reason; instinctive

institutionalization \in''sti tü´ shən əl ī zā´shən\ placement in a residential institution; the process of becoming so adapted to institutional life that one fears leaving

insulin \in''sə lin\ a hormone that is involved in glucose metabolism (commercially prepared and used in the treatment of diabetes)

insulin shock \in´sə lin shok\ collapse reaction to low blood sugar as a result of excessive insulin

insult \in´sult\ in medicine, refers to a trauma

integration \in''tə grā´shən\ harmonious interaction of parts to form a whole; not being segregated

intellect \in´təl lekt\ ability to understand, reason and meet new situations

intelligence \in tel´i jens\ hypothetical construct that refers to an individual's ability to perceive, understand and adapt to his environment

intelligence quotient \in tel´i jens kwō´shənt\ (IQ) score applicable to the interpretation of intelligence obtained from the formula:

$$IQ = \frac{\text{mental age}}{\text{chronological age}} \times 100$$

intelligence tests \in tel´i jens tests\ evaluative instruments designed to measure a person's capacity for learning and adaption

interdisciplinary \in''tėr di´si pli när''ē\ describes the use of different professions such as in the education and treatment of handicapped children

intermittent reinforcement \in''tėr mit´ənt rē''in fôrs´mənt\ selected reward of responses as opposed to continuous reinforcement

interocular \in''tėr ok´ū lėr\ situated between the eyes

intersensory \in''tėr sen´ sə rē\ the use of two or more senses during a learning process

intersensory integration \in''tėr sen´sə rē in''tə grā´shən\ efficient interaction and functioning between two or more senses during a learning process

intersex \in´tėr seks''\ hermaphroditism

interstitial keratitis \in''tėr stish´əl kär´i tī''tis\ chronic inflammation of the cornea that is usually associated with congenital syphilis

intonation \in''tō nā´shən\ rise and fall of voice pitch in speech

intoxication \in''tok´sə kā´shən\ poisoning

intracranial \in''trə krā´nē əl\ within the cranium

intracranial calcification \in''trə krā´nē əl kal''si fi kā´shən\ calcium deposits within the brain; frequently noted among the neurocutaneous syndromes, especially tuberous sclerosis

intraocular \in''trə ok´ū lėr\ within the eye

intrauterine \in''trə ū´tėr in\ within the uterus

intrauterine damage \in''trə ū´tėr in dam´əj\ fetal damage during pregnancy

intropunitive \in''trə pū´ni tiv\ tendency to direct hostility inward; to blame one's self

introspection \in''trə spek´shən\ self-

63

examination of one's own feelings, motivations or mental processes

introvert \in´trə vėrt´´\ person who tends to seek minimal interaction with others

intumescence \in´´tü mes´əns\ the swelling process

in utero \in ū´tə rō\ inside the uterus

invalidism \in´´və lid´´iz əm\ chronic ill health

inversion \in vėr´shən\ structural chromosomal aberration characterized by the rearrangement (reversal) of a portion of gene structure; the 180° rotation of a letter or design while copying or writing

invert \in´vėrt\ a person who directs his sexual interests toward someone of the same sex; a homosexual

involution \in´və lü´shən\ the physical and mental decline that accompanies the aging process

involutional psychosis \in´´və lü´shən əl sī kō´sis\ mental disorder related to middle age characterized by anxiety, depression, worry and hypochondriasis

iodine-[131] \ī´ə dīn´´-[131]\ radioactive isotope of iodine used as measure of thyroid function

iophobia \ī´´ə fō´bē ə\ chronic, unreasonable fear of poisons or of being poisoned

ipsilateral \ip´´si la´tėr əl\ occurring on the same side

iridocyclitis \ėr´´i dō si klī´təs\ inflammation of the iris and ciliary body

iridology \ėr´´i dol´ə jē\ the study of the iris and its characteristics

iridoplegia \i rid´´ə plē´jē ə\ paralysis of the iris so that it does not dilate or contract properly

iris \ī´ris\ circular pigmented membrane that is located behind the cornea of the eye and functions to adjust the amount of light that may enter through the pupil

iritis \i rī´tis\ inflammation of the iris

irradiate \i rā´dē āt´´\ treat or expose to radiation

Ishihari color plates \ish´´i ha´rē kul´ėr plāts\ colored designs used to detect color blindness

isochromosome \i´´sə krō´mə sōm´´\ abnormal chromosome arising through a misdivision at the centromere

isoimmunization \ī´´sō im´´yə nī zā´shən\ process of an organism's developing antibodies against antigens derived from a source within the same species

isolate \ī´sə lāt´´\ individual rejected by peers; separation from others because of contagious disease

isolation \ī´´sə lā´shən\ tendency to remain alone, avoid others

J **jacksonian epilepsy** \jak sō´nē ən ep´ə lep´´sē\ focal epilepsy characterized by localized spasms with a "march" to other areas; usually on the same side, although the seizures may spread to the other side of the body

jactation \jak tā´shən\ stereotyped rocking movements; bragging; also jactitation

jargon \jär´gən\ verbal behavior of young children (nine to eighteen months old); language behavior characteristic of a particular trade or group

jaundice \jŏn´dis\ yellow appearance of the skin due to hyperbilirubinemia

joint \joint\ the point of union between bones

Jukes \jūks\ pseudonym for a well-known family of social misfits

juvenile amaurotic family idiocy \jü´və nīl am´´ô rot´ik fam´i le id´ē ə sē\ Batten-Mayou, Spielmeyer-Vogt syndromes

juvenile delinquent \jü´və nīl dē ling´kwent\ minor not controlled by parental authority and hence in social conflict

juvenilism \jü´və nil´´iz əm\ the persistence of adolescent traits past their appropriate time of life

K **Kallikak** \kal´i kak\ pseudonym of a family described as having two branches, one of superior intelligence and accomplishment, the other mentally retarded and backward

Kanner's syndrome \kan´ėrz sin´drōm\ infantile autism

karyotype \kâr´ē ō tīp´\ orderly arrangement of chromosomes from a single cell

katabolism \kə tab´ə liz´´əm\ catabolism

Kayser-Fleischer ring \kī´zėr flī´shėr ring\ ring of pigmentation, gray and green in color, found on the outer edge of the cornea and related to copper deposits

keloplasty \kē´lō plas´´tē\ plastic surgery to remove a scar

kenophobia \ken´´ə fō´bē ə\ fear of wide open places; agoraphobia

keratitis \kâr´´ə tī´tis\ inflammation of the cornea

keratoconus \kăr´´ə tō kō´nəs\ cone-shaped corneal deformity

keratolgia \kâr´´ə tol´jə\ pain in the corneal area

kernicterus \kėr nik´tėr əs\ yellow staining of the basal ganglia due to hyperbilirubinemia

keratoplasty \kâr´ ə tō plas´´tē\ corneal graft

ketone bodies \kē´tōn bo´dēz\ metabolic byproducts that may be found in the blood and urine in high amounts in conditions such as uncontrolled diabetes

ketonemia \kē´´tō nē´mē ə\ condition of excessive ketone bodies in the blood

ketonuria \kē´´tō nėr´ē ə\ condition of excessive ketone bodies in the urine

kinephantom \kin´´ə fan´təm\ misinterpretation of perceived motion

kinesiology \ki nē´´zē ol´ə jē\ scientific study of human motion

kinesthesia \kin´´əs thē´zhə\ sensory recognition of weight, motion and position by special receptors in the muscles and joints

kinesthetic method \kin´´əs thet´ik meth´əd\ reading technique in which students trace the letters as they read to enhance comprehension

kinetochore \ki net´ə kôr\ centromere

kinship \kin´ship\ family relationship, usually by blood but also by marriage and adoption

Kleeblatschadel syndrome \klē´´blät shä´dəl sin´drōm\ cranial defect due to craniostenosis that results in grotesque skull deformity and mental retardation

kleptomania \klep´´tə mā´nē ə\ compulsion to steal in the absence of economic or social need

kleptophobia \klep´´tə fō´bē ə\ unusual fear of being unable to control urges to steal; overwhelming fear of having possessions stolen

Klinefelter's syndrome \klin´fel tėrz sin´drōm\ 47 XXY chromosome aberration generally characterized by increased height, sterility and possible mental retardation

knee jerk reflex \nē jərk rē´fleks\ automatic forward movement of leg when tapped on patellar tendon

koinoniphobia \koi nō´´ni fō´bē ə\ chronic dread of being in crowded rooms or buildings

kopophobia \kop´´ə fō´bē ə\ chronic, unreasonable fear of becoming overtired

Korsakoff's psychosis \kôr´sə kofs sī kō´sis\ psychosis due to alcoholism characterized by memory defects, disorientation and language disorder

Kufs' disease \kufs di zēz´\ late juvenile cerebral lipidosis

kurtosis \kėr tō´sis\ describes the relative height of a curve that depicts a frequency distribution

kwashiorkor \kwash´´ē ôr´kôr\ disease mainly of the tropics and subtropics characterized by wasting, pigmentation changes and apathy due to prolonged protein-calorie malnutrition; permanent mental retardation or even death may result in more severe cases

kyphoscoliosis \kī´´fō skō´´ lē ō´sis\ condition in which the spine is

kyphosis

abnormally curved both laterally and posteriorly

kyphosis \kī fō´sis\ increase in the posterior or convex curvature of the spine

L **labial** \lā´bē əl\ referring to a lip

labialism \lā´bē əl iz´´əm\ speech defect involving labial sounds

labile \lā´ bil\ unstable

labiology \lā´´bē ol´ə jē\ study of lip movement

labiomancy \lā´bē ō man´´sē\ lipreading; speechreading

labyrinth \lab´ə rinth\ inner ear mechanism involved in hearing and equilibrium

lacrimal \lak´rə məl\ referring to tears

lacrimal sac \lak´rə məl sak\ enlarged upper portion of the lacrimal duct

lacrimal gland \lak´rə məl gland\ gland that secretes tears

lacrimation \lak´´rə mā´shən\ crying, tear production

lactation \lak tā´shən\ milk production

lagerity \lə jėr´i tē\ physical or mental agility

lagophthalmos \lag´´of thal´mōs\ condition in which the eyelids cannot be completely closed

laliophobia \lal´´ē ə fō´bē ə\ refusal to speak for fear of stuttering; lalophobia

lall \lal\ defective production of *l* and *r* sounds

lallation \lə lā´shən\ babble; meaningless speech; speech in which the *l* sound is substituted for sounds that are harder to produce

lalopathy \lal op´ə thē\ speech disorder

lalophobia \lal´´ə fō´bē ə\ laliophobia

laloplegia \lal´´ə plē´jē ə\ speech incapacity due to muscle paralysis

lame \lām\ injured or disabled in the hip, leg or foot so as to cause a limp in walking

language \lang´gwidj\ vocal or other means of expressing or communicating thought or feeling

laryngectomy \lär´´ən jek´tə mē\ surgical removal of the larynx

laryngology \lär´´ing gol´ə jē\ medical specialty concerned with the pharynx and upper pulmonary tree

laryngoscope \lär ing´gə skōp\ apparatus used for visual examination of the larynx

larynx \lär´ingks\ organ of the voice

laser cane \lā´zėr kān\ infrared device used by the blind to detect obstacles

latah \lä´tə\ psychiatric impairment characterized by tics, foul language, imitation of the behavior of others; found chiefly in the Orient; same as Gilles de la Tourette's syndrome

latent \lā´tənt\ inactive or hidden characteristic or trait that has the potential to become manifested

lateral \lat´ér əl\ refers to the outer side; away from the median

laterality \lat´´ə ral´i tē\ preferential use of sense organs and extremities of one side of the body

Laurence-Moon-Biedl syndrome \lôr´ens - mün - bē´dəl sin´drōm\ hereditary mental retardation syndrome characterized by sexual infantilism, obesity, visual defects and cardiovascular abnormalities

lead arsenate \led är´sə nāt´\ compound of lead and arsenic widely used as a pesticide

lead poisoning \led poi´zən ing\ plumbism; a condition due to ingestion or inhalation of lead or certain lead compounds that may result in neurological impairment and death

learning curve \lėr´ning kėrv\ graphic representation of successive performances

learning disabilities \lėr´ning dis´´ə bil´i tēz\ specific disorder or retardation in one of the following: language, perception, speech, behavior, reading, writing, spelling or arithmetic; not due to mental retardation, emotional problems, disadvantaged environment or hearing, motor or visual handicaps

Legg-Calvé-Perthes disease \leg-cavpėrth´ēz di zēz´\ a crippling bone disorder involving the head of the femur

lenition \li nish´ən\ weakening of a consonant sound

lens \lenz\ refractive medium used to focus or disperse light rays

lenticular \len tik´ū lėr\ referring to a lens

leptocephalia \lep´´tō sə fä´lē ə\ abnormal tallness of the head

leptophonia \lep´´tə fō´nē ə\ weakness of the voice

leptosomic \lep´´tə sōm´ik\ referring to a person of thin, slight body type

leresis \lə rē´sis\ garrulousness of the aged

lesbianism \lez´bē ən iz´´əm\ homosexuality among females

Lesch-Nyhan syndrome \lesh-nī´ən sin´drōm\ hereditary (X-linked) disorder characterized by cerebral palsy, mental retardation, self-mutilation and hyperuricemia

lesion \lē´zhən\ damage to tissue due to injury or disease

lethal \lē´thəl\ referring to that which causes death

lethal gene \lē´thəl jēn\ gene that when expressed results in the death of the organism

lethargy \leth´ér jē\ an abnormal state of drowsiness or apathy

lethe \lē´thē\ amnesia; forgetfulness

lethologica \leth´ə lō´ji kə\ condition in which one cannot remember the proper word to be used

leucocyte \lü´kə sīt\ white blood cell; leukosite

leukemia \lü kē´mē ə\ a group of diseases of blood-forming tissues

leukocytosis \lü´´kō sī tō´sis\ increased number of white cells in the blood

leukopenia \lü´´kə pē´nē ə\ decreased number of white cells in the blood

leveling \lev´əl ing\ phenomena in which perceptions are recalled as more regular, more symmetrical than they actually are

libidinous \li bid´i nəs\ lustful

libido \li bē´ dō\ basic drives of the id; specifically, the sexual drive

ligament \lig´ə mənt\ tough, connective, fibrous band uniting bone to bone

light adaption \līt ə dap´shən\ ability of the eye to adjust to varying amounts of light; light adaptation

light perception \līt pér sep´shən\ ability of the eyes to discriminate light from dark

limbus \lim´bəs\ boundary between the cornea and sclera, also called corneal limbus

lineage \lin´ē əj\ direct, traceable descent from an ancestor

linguadental \ling´gwə den´´təl\ refers to sounds produced with the aid of the tongue and the teeth

lingual \ling´gwəl\ pertaining to the tongue

linguistics \ling gwis´tiks\ science of language

linkage \ling´kij\ association of genetic factors due to the genes being in the same chromosome; association of a genetic factor with a certain chromosome, especially the sex chromosome

linked \lingkt\ refers to characteristics that are always inherited together

lipidosis \li´´pi do´sis\ disorders of lipid metabolism

lipids \lip´idz\ various types of fats

lipochondrodystrophy \lip´´ə kon´´drō dis´trə fē\ Hurler's syndrome, mucopolysaccharidosis I

lipreading \lip rēd´ing\ comprehending speech of another through the visual interpretation of gestures, facial movements and especially lip movements; speechreading

lisp \lisp\ incorrect pronunciation of the sibilant sounds *s, z, sh, ch,* and *j*

literacy \lit´er ə sē\ ability to read and write as measured by an arbitrary standard

Little's disease \lit´əls di zēz\ cerebral palsy

liveness \līv´nəs\ acoustical term used to describe the fidelity of sound in a particular room or area

load \lōd\ the number of cases handled by a person in a helping profession

lobe \lōb\ round projection of an organ; especially used to describe a part of the outer ear or one of the five parts of the cerebrum

lobectomy \lō bek´tə mē\ surgical removal of parts of the brain; used in the treatment of mental illness

lobotomy \lō bot´ə mē\ severing of

nerve pathways of the brain for the treatment of mental illness

locus \lō′kəs\ position of a gene on a chromosome

logagraphia \lō′′gə graf′ē ə\ inability to express one's self in writing

logokophosis \lō′′gə kə fō′sis\ inability to understand verbal language

logopathy \lō gop′ə thē\ speech defect related to central nervous system disorders

logopedics \lo′′gə pē′diks\ science dealing with speech defects

logoplegia \lō′′gə plē′jē ə\ paralysis of speech organs; inability to speak due to paralysis

logorrhea \lō′′gə rē′ə\ uncontrollable, excessive loud talking

lordosis \lôr dō′ sis\ type of spinal curvature; swayback

loudness \loud′nəs\ intensity of sound

love \luv\ strong affection or attachment

lucidity \lü sid′ i tē\ clearness; time period between insane lapses

lues \lü′ēz\ syphilis

lumbar \lum′bär\ area dealing with loins or lower back

lumbar puncture \lum′bär punk′chèr\ the withdrawal of cerebrospinal fluid with a needle in the lumbar region; used for diagnostic purposes

lunacy \lün′ ə sē\ insanity or craziness; obsolete term

lust \lust\ immoderate or illicit craving

lymph \limf\ a clear, alkaline liquid of the lymphatic system

lymphangioma \limf an′′jē ō′mə\ tumor composed of vessels that contain lymph

lymphedema \lim′′fə dē′mə\ swelling of extremities usually caused by excess of lymph due to lymph vessel blockage

lymphoma \lim fō′mə\ tumor of lymphoid tissue

lypemania \lī′′pə mā′nē ə\ abnormal, prolonged depression

lysergic acid diethylamide \li sèr′jik as′id dī eth′əl ə mīd′′\ LSD, a hallucinogenic drug

M **macrencephaly** \mak´´ren sef´ə lē\ hyperplasia of the brain; macrencephalia

macrobiotic \mak´rō bī´ot ik\ pertaining to organisms visible to the unaided eye

macrocephaly \mak´´rō sef´ə lē\ abnormally large head, usually associated with low intelligence

macrocrania \mak´´rō krā´nē ə\ abnormally large skull size in the presence of normally sized facial area

macrodontia \mak´´rə don´shə\ abnormally large teeth

macrogyria \mak´´rō jē´rē ə\ a congenital defect characterized by unusually large cerebral convolutions

macrophthalmous \mak´´rəf thal´məs\ abnormally large eyes

macroplasia \mak´´rō plā´zhə\ overgrowth of tissue on a body part

macropsia \mə krop´sē ə\ visual defect in which objects are perceived as being larger than their actual size; megalopsia

macula \mak´yə lə\ a yellow-stained area surrounding the fovea of the eye that comprises the most acute area of vision; the complete term for this area of the eye is macula lutea retinae

madhouse \mad´hous\ colloquial for mental hospital

madness \mad´nəs\ insanity

mainstreaming \mān strēm´ing\ process of placing handicapped students in regular classes

malacia \mə lā´shə\ morbid softening of an organ, tissue or body part; abnormal craving for spicy food

maladaptive \mal´´ə dap´tiv\ defective or reduced ability to adjust to environmental demands

maladjustment \mal´´ə just´mənt\ defective environmental adaptation characterized by anxiety, instability and depression

malaise \ma lāz´\ discomfort or weakness at the onset of illness; general, nonfocused feeling of uneasiness

malformation \mal´´fôr mā´shən\ physical defect due to defective development

malfunction \mal funk´shən\ the breakdown of a part or a system

malignant \mə lig´nənt\ virulent and deadly

malinger \mə ling´gėr\ to fake symptoms of illness or disability

malleus \mal´ē əs\ largest of the three auditory bones in the middle ear, attached to the ear drum; the hammer

malnutrition \mal´´nü trish´ən\ disorders related to insufficient or defective diet

malpractice \mal prak´tis\ failure of a teacher, psychologist, physician or other professional person to deliver adequate service through negligence or intent

malpresentation \mal´´prēz en tā´shən\ abnormal or dangerous fetal positioning at time of birth; malposition

mandible \man´di bəl\ bone forming lower jaw

mandibular \man dib´ū lėr\ pertaining to the mandible

mania \mā´nē ə\ abnormal preoccupation with an idea, desire or activity

maniaphobia \mā´´nē ə fō´bē ə\ unreasonable fear of becoming mentally ill

manic \man´ik\ affected by mania; hyperactive; excitable

manic-depressive \man´ik di pres´iv\ type of behavior characterized by swings between periods of excitement and hyperactivity and periods of depression and lethargy

manipulation \mə nip´ū lā´shən\ the use of the hands or other body parts to move objects; the use of indirect or covert methods to control the behavior of others

mannerism \man´ə riz´´əm\ identifiable recurring movement, gesture or behavior

manual dominance \man´ū əl dom´i nəns\ preference for the use of one hand over the other

maple syrup urine disease \mā´pəl sėr´əp yėr´ən di zēz´\ hereditary, progressive disease characterized by early neurological deterioration, cerebral palsy, convulsions, mental retardation and odor of maple syrup from urine

marasmus \mə raz′məs\ wasting away due to malnutrition

Marfan's syndrome \mär′fanz sin′drōm\ hereditary disorder characterized by abnormally long fingers and toes, slender body build, eye and cardiovascular problems

Marie's ataxia \mə rēz′ ə tak′sē ə\ hereditary cerebellar ataxia

masculinization \mas′′kū li nī zā′shən\ the development of male secondary sex characteristics in a female

mask \mask\ in audiometry, a technique of concealing one sound by simultaneously emitting another sound of a differing frequency

masochism \mas′ə kiz′′əm\ deriving enjoyment from being mistreated or seeking mistreatment to gratify sexual needs

massotherapy \mas′′ō thăr′ə pē\ medical treatment of a condition by massage

mastoiditis \mas′′toid ī′tis\ inflammation of the mastoid process

masturbation \mas′′tėr bā′shən\ self-stimulation of genitals for sexual gratification

maternal \mə tėr′nəl\ pertaining to the mother

maturation \ma′′chə rā′shən\ developmental process of an organism

maxilla \mak sil′ə\ one of two bones composing the upper jaw

mean \mēn\ average of two or more values

measles \mē′zelz\ contagious viral infection

measure \mā′zhėr\ to determine the quantity or limits of something; the extent, quantity or degree

measured intelligence \māzh′ėrd in tel′i jens\ rating of intelligence by using standardized general intelligence tests such as the Stanford-Binet and the Wechsler series

medial \mē′dē əl\ midway or toward the center

median \mē′dē ən\ the midpoint of a frequency distribution

medical \med′i kəl\ pertaining to medicine

medicate \med′i kāt′\ to affect with medicine

medicine \med′i sən\ a drug or chemical used to treat or heal

medium \mē′dē um\ a substance that holds or transmits something else

megacephaly \meg′′ə sef′ə lē\ megalocephaly

megalocephaly \meg′′ə lō sef′ə lē\ abnormally large head, including calvarium and facial bones; megacephaly

megalomania \meg′′ə lō mā′nē ə\ chronic overevaluation of one's own worth; delusions of grandeur

megalophthalmos \meg′′ə lōf thal′mōs\ macrophthalmos; abnormally large eyes; megalopia

megalopsia \meg′′ə lop′sē ə\ macropsia

megavitamin therapy \meg′′ə vī′tə min thăr′ə pē\ the administration of extremely large doses of specific vitamins with the expectation of improving health or behavior

meiosis \mī ō′sis\ a type of cell division that results in the formation of the gametes

melancholia \mel′′ən kō′le ə\ chronic state of depression, sadness, low self-esteem and decreased sensitivity to environmental stimulation without apparent cause

melanin \mel′ə nin\ dark pigment that gives the various shades of tan, brown and black to human skin, hair and eye coloration

melanoma \mel′′ə nō′mə\ tumor of the skin or eyes

melioristic \mel′yə ris′′tik\ tending toward improvement

melomania \mel′′ə mā′nē ə\ obsessive preoccupation with music

membrane \mem′brān\ thin layer of tissue covering surface of an organ

memory \mem′ə rē\ the faculty that permits recall of previous perceptions, observations and sensations

memory span \mem′ə rē span\ amount

of information one can recall immediately after the material is presented

menalgia \mə näl´jə\ painful menstruation

menarche \mə när´kē\ the first menstral flow in the female

meninges \me nin´jēz\ the membranes that cover the brain and spinal cord

meningitis \men´´in jī´təs\ inflammation of the meninges

meningocele \mə ning´gō sēl\ projection of the meninges from the skull or spinal column

meningoencephalitis \mə ning´´gō en sef´´ə lī´tis\ inflammation of the meninges and brain in combination

meningoencephalomyelopathy \mə ning´´gō en sef´´ə lō mī´´ ə lop´ ə thē\ damage resulting from disease affecting meninges, brain and spinal cord

menopause \men´ə päz\ change of life or cessation of menstruation in females past the reproductive age

menses \men´sēz\ menstrual discharge

mental \men´təl\ referring to the mind

mental age \men´təl   āj\ level of intellectual development equivalent to the average of a particular chronological age group, usually as reflected in test scores

mental defective \men´təl dē fekt´iv\ mentally retarded person

mental deficiency \men´təl di fish´ən sē\ mental retardation

mental deterioration \men´təl dē tēr´ē ə rā´´shən\ regression in the level of intellectual functioning and in the level or organization and control of behavior

mental disease \men´təl di´zēz\ any of the neuroses or psychoses

mental factor \men´təl fak´tėr\ variable considered in an investigation of mental capacity

mental growth \men´təl grōth\ changes in intelligence associated with normal growth and development

mental handicap \men´təl   han´dē kap´´\ sometimes used as a synonym of mental retardation, also used to refer to a specific defect in intelligence

mental hygiene \men´təl hī´jēn\ measures to reduce mental illness through prevention and early treatment; maintenance of healthy emotional responses and prevention of development of mental instability

mental retardation \men´təl   rē´´tär dā´shən\ defined by the American Association of Mental Deficiency as significant subaverage general intellectual functioning existing concurrently with deficits in adaptive behavior, and manifested during the development period.

mental   subnormality   \men´təl sub´´nôr mal´i tē\ degree to which the individual's intellectual capacity is below normal

mercurialism \mėr kyūr´ē ə liz´´əm\ the state of being poisoned by mercury

meropia \mə rō´pē ə\ partial sightedness

mesocephalic \mez´´ō sə fal´ik\ having a head configuration midway between brachycephaly and dolichocephaly

mesomorph \mez´ə môrf´´\ athletic body type

metabolic disease \met´´ə bol´ik di zēz´\ disease or condition caused by malfunction of a particular metabolic process that results in a fairly typical symptomatology

metabolism \mə tab´ə liz´´əm\ the processes by which food substances are changed into living tissue and this matter is transformed into energy and wastes

metacarpal \met´´ə kär´pəl\ bones between wrists and fingers

metalanguage \met´´ə lang´gwij\ part of a language that describes the rules for its use

metamorphosis \met´´ə môr´fə sis\ dramatic change or transformation

metaphase \met´ə fāz´´\ phase of cell division that is characterized by the disappearance of the nuclear membrane and the formation of the spindle

methemoglobinemia \meth´´ē mō glō´´bi nē´mē ə\ a toxic state in which hemoglobin molecules have bonded with nitrites causing cyanosis in the affected individual

methodology \meth´´ə dol´ə jē\ the systematic utilization of methods; the principles governing scientific procedures for study and research

methomania \meth´´ə mā´nē ə\ mental instability or derangement as a result of chronic alcoholism

micrencephalous \mī´´kren sef´ə ləs\ a person having a small brain

micrencephaly \mī´´kren sef´ə lē\ abnormally small brain

microbiology \mī´´krō bī ol´ə je\ study of microorganisms

microcephalus \mī´´krō sef´ə ləs\ person with an abnormally small head

microcephaly \mī´´krō sef´ə lē\ condition characterized by a very small head and mental retardation

microdontia \mī´´krō don´shə \ abnormally small teeth

micrognathia \mī´´krō nā´thē ə\ unusually small jaw; receding chin

microgyria \mī´´krō jī´rē ə\ abnormally small cerebral convolutions

micromelia \mī´´krō mē´lē ə\ abnormally small limbs

microphobia \mī´´krə fō´bē ə\ unreasonable, chronic fear of microorgranisms

microphonia \mī´´krə fō´nē ə\ marked vocal weakness

microphthalmus \mī´´krof thal´məs\ abnormally small eyes; microphthalmia

microplasia \mī´´krə plā´zhə\ dwarfism

micropsia \mī krop´sē ə\ visual defect in which objects are perceived as smaller than their actual size

micturate \mik´chə rāt´´\ urinate

middle ear \mid´əl ēr\ the part of the ear that contains the hammer, anvil and stirrup

migraine \mī´grān\ severe headache, usually confined to one side of the

head and possibly accompanied by nausea

milieu \mil yū´\ environmental medium; ecosystem

milieu therapy \mil yū´ thăr´ə pē\ treatment based upon consideration of environmental forces and parameters

mimic gene \mim´ik jēn\ genes producing apparently identical results

mimicry \mim´ik rē\ imitation of actions, speech or facial expressions of another individual

minimal brain damage \min´ə məl brān dam´əj\ minor central nervous system dysfunction that may manifest in a learning disability

miosis \mī ō´sis\ meiosis (genetics); in vision, refers to contraction of the pupil

miotic drug \mī ot´ik drug\ agent that contracts the pupil of the eye

mirror reversal \měr´ěr rē věrs´ əl\ reversing letters or symbols in reading as though seen in a mirror, such as *b* for *d*

mirror writing \měr´ěr rīt´ing\ writing that is reversed, as though seen in a mirror

misanthropia \mis´´ən thrō´pē ə\ hatred of humanity

miscegenation \mi´´sej ə nā´ shən\ reproduction by persons of differing racial background

misogamy \mi sog´ə mē\ strong dislike and avoidance of marriage

misogyny \mi soj´ə nē\ hatred of women

misopedia \mī´´sə pē´dē ə\ hatred of children

mitosis \mī tō´sis\ the cell division of growth

mitotic \mī tot´ik\ pertaining to mitosis

mixed dominance \mikst dom´ə nəns\ lack of consistent lateral dominance

mixoscopia \mik´´sə skō´pē ə\ voyeurism

mnemonic \ni mon´ik\ of the memory

modality \mō dal´i tē\ one of the five senses: hearing, vision, touch, taste or smell; a method of application in physiotherapy

mode \mōd\ in statistics, the point in a frequency distribution that indicates the highest rate of occurrence

modeling \mod´ə ling\ providing an example of a desired behavior

modifying genes \mod´ə fī´´ing jēns\ genetic factor that alters the action of other genes

module \mo´jūl\ a standard unit or subunit of a larger design

mogiphonia \mō´´jə fō´nē ə\ voice strain that causes speaking difficulty

momism \mom´iz əm\ excessive dependence upon maternal care and protection

monaural \mon ôr´əl\ pertaining to or involving one ear

mongolism \mon´gə liz´´əm\ Down's syndrome; mongoloid; mongol; congenital acromicria

monobulia \mon´´ō bü´lē ə\ abnormal preoccupation with a single desire or wish

monochorionic \ mon´´ō kôr´´ē on´ ik\ twin embryos sharing a single chorion

monocular \mə nok´yə lér\ having to do with one eye

monogamy \mon ô´gə mē\ the marriage of one man to one woman

monomania \mon´´ə mā´nē ə\ preoccupation with one subject, idea or activity

monopathophobia \mon´´ō path´´ə fō´bē ə\ abnormal fear of a particular disease

monophobia \mon´´ō fō´bē ə\ abnormal fear of being alone

monopitch \mon´ō pitch\ speech with limited inflection

monoplegia \mon´´ə plē´jē ə\ paralysis of a single limb

monosomy \mon ə sō´mē\ condition of having only one of a chromosome pair

monotone \mon´ə tōn\ voice quality having a limited pitch variability

monozygous twins \mon´´ə zī´gəs twinz\ two identical siblings produced by a single fertilized ovum

monster \mon´stér\ grossly deformed infant

Moore's syndrome \môrz sin´drōm\ abdominal epilepsy

morbid \môr´bid\ unhealthy, pathological, defective

morbidity rate \môr bid´i tē rāt\ ratio of infants born with defects compared to total live births; ratio of sick persons to well

mores \môr´āz\ the ethical sanctions of a culture

moribund \môr´i bund´´\ close to death; dying

moron \môr´on\ person in the mild range of mental retardation

Moro's reflex \môr´ōz rē´fleks\ reflex observed in infants up to six months consisting of a concussion reaction that can be elicited by sudden noise or upsetting the equilibrium; also called startle reflex

morpheme \môr´fēm\ the smallest language unit that has a meaning of its own, such as the words cat, tree, fall and two

morphology \môr fol´ə jē\ form and structure of bodies

mortality rate \môr tal´i tē rāt\ ratio of deaths from a disease or condition compared to the total afflicted

mosaicism \mō zā´i siz´´əm\ genetic abnormality in which an individual has cells of different chromosome complements

motivation \mō´´tə vā´shən\ reasons that induce a person to act in a certain way

motor \mō´tér\ referring to movement

motor aphasia \mō´tér ə fā´ zhə\ speech defect due to neuromuscular incoordination

motor dysfunction \mō´tér dis funk´shən\ defect in movement

mucopolysaccharidosis \mū´´kō pol´´ē sak´´ə rī dō´sis\ defects of polysaccharide metabolism

multifactorial \mul´´tē fak tôr´ē əl\ resulting from many sources; in genetics, resulting from the interaction of more than two genes

multiple birth \mul´tə pəl bérth\ a pregnancy and delivery that result in two or more offspring

multiple gene characteristic \mul´tə pəl jēn kăr´´ək tə ris´tik\ characteristic produced by a number of genes that combine with each other to produce an additive effect

multiple personality \mul´tə pəl pėr´´sə nal´i tē\ two or more separate personality systems within one person

multiple sclerosis \mul´tə pəl sklə rō´sis\ progressive disease of the central nervous system characterized by weakness, spasticity and incoordination, occurring mostly in young adults

multiply handicapped \mul´ti plē han´dē kapt´´\ having handicaps in more than one area, such as mental retardation, vision and hearing defects

multisensory learning \mul´´ti sen´sə rē lėrn´ing\ combining of sense modalities to facilitate learning

muscle spasm \mus´əl spaz´əm\ muscular contraction that is involuntary

muscular atrophy \mus´kū lėr a´trə fē\ reduction in muscle tissue

muscular coordination \mus kū lėr kō ôr´´ də nā´shən\ working together of parts of the body harmoniously

muscular dystrophy \mus´kū lėr dis´trə fē\ progressive wasting disease of the muscles

musculature \mus´kū lə chėr\ all the muscles of the body or of a part

musicomania \mū´si kō mā´nē ə\ abnormal fondness of music; melomania; musomania

musophobia \mū´´sō fō´bē ə\ chronic, unreasonable fear of mice and other small rodents

mutagen \mū´tə jən\ agent that causes mutations

mutagenesis \mū´´tə jen´ə sis\ the process of producing a mutation

mutation \mū tā´shən\ change in a gene's effect

mute \mūt\ unable or unwilling to speak

mutism \mū´tiz əm\ condition characterized by inability or unwillingness to speak

muton \mū´ton\ smallest part of genetic material

mutualism \mū´chū əl iz´´əm\ symbiotic dependence between two individuals, groups or species

myalgia \mī al´jə\ muscular pain

myasthenia \mī´´əs thē´nē ə\ muscular weakness

myasthenia gravis \mī´´əs thē´´nē ə gra´vis\ syndrome characterized by weakness, fatigue and progressive paralysis

myatonia \mī´´ə tō´nē ə\ decreased muscle tone and strength

myatrophy \mī a´trə fē\ decrease in muscle size and strength

mydriatic drug \mī´´drē a´tik drug\ agent that dilates the pupil of the eye

myelin \mī´ə lin\ sheath around nerve fibers

myelitis \mī´´ə lī´tis\ inflammation of spinal cord

myelomeningocele \mī´´ə lo mə ning´gə sēl\ a sac containing part of a malformed spinal cord and meninges that protrudes from a defect in the spinal column

myeloplegia \mī´´ə lō plē´jē ə\ paralysis of the spine

myocarditis \mī´´ō kär dī´tis\ inflammation of a heart muscle

myoclonic seizures \mī´´ō klōn´ik sē´zhėrz\ sudden, short, generalized muscle contractions in infants

myogenesis \mī´ō jen´ə sis\ formation of muscle tissue

myology \mi ol´ō jē\ the study of muscles, their function and disorders

myopathy \mī op´ə thē\ damage or disease of muscle tissue

myopia \mī ō´pē ə\ nearsighted; a refractive error in which light rays focus in front of the retina

myosis \mī´ō sis\ miosis

myositis \mī´´ə sī´tis\ inflammation of the muscles

myotonia \mī´´ə tō´nē ə\ increased muscle tension associated with spasms and pain

myotonic dystrophy \mī˝ə tōn´ik
dis´trə fē\ form of muscular dystrophy; Steinert's disease
mysophilia \mī˝sə fil´ē ə\ chronic,
morbid fascination with filth
mysophobia \mī˝sə fō´bē ə\ chronic,
unreasonable fear of dirt or contamination by germs
myxedema \mik˝si dē´mə\ a condition
due to lack of thyroid secretion
marked by lethargy, dullness and
infiltration of the skin by edema

N **nanism** \nan´iz əm\ dwarfism
nanocephaly \nan´´ə sef´ə lē\ abnormal smallness of head

nanomelia \na´´nə mē´lē ə\ abnormal smallness of the arms and legs

nanosoma \na´´nə sō´mə\ unusually small body; nanism; nanosomia

narcissism \när´si siz´´əm\ love of self

narcoanalysis \när´´kō ə nal´i sis\ use of drugs during psychiatric treatment to improve recall of repressed feelings or memories

narcolepsy \när´kə lep´´sē\ condition characterized by intermittent attacks of sleepiness

narcoma \när kō´mə\ state of lethargy or stupor produced by drugs

narcomania \när´´kō mā´nē ə\ irresistible desire for alcohol or narcotics

narcosis \när kō´sis\ state of being under the influence of narcotic drugs

narcosomania \när´´kō sə ma´nē ə\ abnormal desire to be narcotized

narcotic \när´ kot´ik\ drug or chemical agent that produces stupor or deadening of the senses

narcotize \när´kə tīz\ to place under the influence of narcotic drugs

nares \när´ēz\ the two nostrils

nasal \nā´zəl\ related to the nose or nasal cavity

nasality \nā sal´i tē\ quality of speech when the nasal cavity is used as a resonator, especially when there is too much nasal resonance

nasal septum \nā´səl sep´təm\ midplane partition separating the two nasal cavities

nascent \nā´sənt\ referring to birth or the beginning of something

natal \nā´təl\ referring to birth

native intelligence \nā´tiv in tel´i jens\ inherited intellect

nearsightedness \nēr sī´tid nəs\ myopia

nearthrosis \nē´´ėr thrō´sis\ artificial joint developed in a bone shaft through surgery

nebula \neb´ū lə\ minor opacity of the cornea

necromania \nek´´rə mā´nē ə\ morbid preoccupation with death

necromimesis \nek´´rō mi mē´sis\ delusional belief that one is dead

necrophilia \nek´´rə fil´ē ə\ sexual interest in corpses

necrophobia \nek´´rə fō´bē ə\ overwhelming fear of death or dead bodies

necrosis \nə krō´sis\ local death of cells

need \nēd\ any basic drive that may motivate an individual to action

negative reinforcement \neg´ə tiv rē´´in fôrs´mənt\ process in which a behavior increases in frequency or is strengthened by having the behavior followed by the removal of a negative stimulus

negative reinforcer \neg´ə tiv rē´´in fôrs´ėr\ aversive stimulus that is removed following a response in order to maintain or increase the response

negativism \neg´ə ti viz´´əm\ propensity to do the opposite of what others wish or expect

negrophobia \nē´´grə fō´bē ə\ strong fear or hatred of blacks

Nemeth code \nē´məth cōd\ braille type system used by the blind in performing mathematical computations

neogenesis \ne´´ō jen´ ə sis\ generation of new knowledge through sensory stimulation and intellectual processing

neologism \nē´´ə lōj´iz əm\ use of new words or symbols whose meanings may be unknown to the reader or listener; meaningless words used by a mentally ill person

neonatal \nē´´ō nā´təl\ first four weeks following birth

neophobia \nē´´ə fō´bē ə\ abnormal fear of new things or experiences

neoplasm \nē´ə plaz´´əm\ tumor

neoplasty \nē´ə plas´´tē\ repair of a body part through plastic surgery

nephelopia \nef´´ə lō´pē ə\ dimness of vision due to corneal clouding

nephritis \nə frī´tis\ kidney inflammation

nerve deafness \nėrv def´nəs\ profound hearing problem due to defective auditory nerve

nervimuscular \nėrv´´ i mus´kyə lėr\ referring to innervation of the muscles

nervous breakdown \nėr´vus brāk´down\ a popular term for a period of mental and emotional dysfunction

neural \nūr´əl\ referring to the nerves

neuralgia \nū ral´jə\ a localized neural defect characterized by sharp pain in the affected area

neurapraxia \nūr´´ə prak´sē ə\ paralysis caused by nerve damage of slight degree, usually reversible

neurasthenia \nūr´´əs thē´nē ə\ chronic fatigue produced by anxiety

neuraxis \nū rak´sis\ spinal cord and brain

neurectomy \nū rek´tə mē\ removal or cutting of a nerve

neuritis \nū rī´tis\ inflammation of a nerve

neurocutaneous syndromes \nūr´´ə kū tā´ nē əs sin´drōmz\ syndromes in which symptomology is present in both the nervous system and the skin

neurofibroma \nūr´´ə fī brōm ə\ tumor of the nerve fibers

neurofibromatosis \nūr´´ə fī´´brō mə tō´sis\ one of the neurocutaneous syndromes; also called Von Recklinghausen's disease

neuroleptic drugs \nūr´´ə lep´tik drugz\ medicines that produce symptoms resembling those of nervous system diseases

neurologically handicapped \nū´´rō loj´i kə lē han´dē kapt´´\ refers to a person with an impairment due to central nervous system defect

neurologist \nū rol´ə jist\ specialist in diagnosis and treatment of nervous disorders

neurology \nūr ol´ə jē\ study of the nervous system, its functioning and diseases

neuromuscular \nūr´´ə mus´kyə lėr\ referring to nerves and muscle

neuron \nūr´on\ nerve cell

neuropathic \nūr´´ə path´ik\ damaging to the nervous system

neuropathology \nūr´´ə path ol´ə jē\ study of diseases of the nervous system and structural or functional changes occurring in them

neurophrenia \nūr´ə frē´nē ə\ learning disability

neurosis \nū rō´sis\ an emotional conflict that reduces the effectiveness of the individual's functioning but in which there is little loss of contact with reality

neurosyphilis \nū´´rō sif´ə lis\ syphilis that affects the central nervous system

neurotigenic \nū rōt´´i jen´ik\ causing or facilitating neurosis

neurotoxin \nūr´´ə tok´sin\ poison that affects the nervous system

neurotropic \nūr´´ə trop´ik\ attracted to the nervous system

nevus \nē´vəs\ skin growth caused by hypertrophy of blood vessels or tissue; includes all moles and some birthmarks

nevus flammeus \nē´vəs flam´ē əs\ capillary hemangioma; also called port wine stain

Niemann-Pick disease \nē´mən-pik di zēz´\ hereditary lipid disorder characterized by rapidly progressive neurological involvement, blindness, mental retardation and early demise

nihilism \nī´ə liz´´əm\ delusion that all is unreal, that nothing really exists

niphablepsia \nif´´ə blep´sē ə\ snow blindness

nitrite poisoning \nī´trīt poi´zə ning\ methemoglobinemia

nociceptor \nō´´si sep´tėr\ a pain receptor

noctambulation \nok´´tam byə lā´shən\ sleepwalking, somnambulism

noctiphobia \nok´´ti fō´bē ə\ fear of darkness or the night; nyctophobia

noctograph \nok´tə graf´´\ writing aid used by the blind

nocturnal \nok tėr´nəl\ pertaining to nighttime

nocturnal emission \nok tėr´nǝl ē mish´ǝn\ wet dream; ejaculation of semen during nighttime sleep

nocturnal enuresis \nok tėr´nǝl en´´yǝ rē´sis\ bedwetting at night

nodule \noj´ül\ small nonbony protuberance or growth

nomadism \nō´mad iz´´ǝm\ pathological wandering

nonambulatory \non am´´bū lǝ tôr´ē\ unable to walk

noncategorical \non ka´´tǝ gôr´ i kǝl\ not classified according to type of handicap

nondirective therapy \non´´di rek´tiv thǎr´ǝ pē\ a client centered method of counselling in which the therapist refrains from directing or evaluating the client's remarks or feelings

nondisjunction \non´´dis jungk´shǝn\ failure during cell division of a chromosome pair to separate

nonfluency \non flü´ǝn sē\ disrhythmic speech

nonparametric \non´´pǎr ǝ me´trik\ refers to statistical procedures that do not assume normal distribution of the data

nonverbal \non vėr´bǝl\ not involving the use of words

norm \nôrm\ average measurement of a large representative group

normal \nôr´mǝl\ agreed upon standard or type; characteristics that fall plus or minus over standard deviation from their mean

normal curve \nôr´mǝl kėrv\ a curve that illustrates the distribution of observations in a normal population

normal distribution \nôr´mǝl dis´´trǝ bū´shǝn\ data scattered in accordance with normal probability

normalization \nôr´´mǝl ī zā´shǝn\ process of bringing within normal limits

norm reference \nôrm ref´ėr ǝns\ the judgment of an individual performance by comparing it to the performance of others

nosology \nō sol´ǝ jē\ classification of diseases

nosomania \nō´´sǝ mā´nē ǝ\ delusion that one has a particular disease

nosophobia \nō´´sǝ fō´bē ǝ\ unreasonable fear of disease

nostomania \nos´´tǝ mā´nē ǝ\ irresistible desire to return home

noxious \nok´shǝs\ harmful

nuclear family \nü´klē ėr fam´i lē\ that related group containing mother, children and usually father

nucleus \nü´klē us\ center

nudomania \nü´´dǝ mā´nē ǝ\ abnormal fear of disrobing, of being nude

null hypothesis \nul hī poth´ǝ sis\ negative statement of a purported truth to be tested

number concept \num´bėr kon´sept\ the construct that enables its possessor to count and use numbers to represent quantity

numeration \nu´´mǝ rā´shǝn\ counting, calculating or otherwise processing numbers

nurture \nėr´chėr\ to provide what is necessary to enhance growth or health

nutation \nü tā´shǝn\ involuntary head nodding

nutrient \nü´trē ǝnt\ a substance that nourishes a body

nutrition \nü tri´shǝn\ processes involved in an organism's growth and maintenance

nyctalopia \nik´´tǝ lō´pē ǝ\ night blindness

nyctophobia \nik´´tǝ fō´bē ǝ\ chronic, unreasonable fear of the dark; noctiphobia

nympholepsy \nim´fǝ lep´´sē\ inappropriate frenzy or ecstasy

nymphomania \nim´´ fǝ mā´nē ǝ\ abnormally strong sex drive in females

nystagmus \ni stag´mǝs\ rapid, involuntary, jerky movement of the eyeball

O **obedience** \ō bē´ dē əns\ compliance with a directive

obesity \ō bēs´i tē\ fat accumulation that is detrimental to health

object blindness \ob´jekt blīnd´nəs\ visual agnosia

object constancy \ob´jekt kon´stən sē\ the ability to perceive certain objects as the same despite differing environmental circumstances

objective techniques \ob jek´tiv tek nēks´\ contrived situations that can be repeated and proved with no preconceived ideas regarding outcomes

objectivity \ob´´jek tiv´i tē\ that which is unaffected by prejudgment or bias

obsequiousness \ob sē´kwē əs nəs\ excessively willing to serve or obey; overly submissive

obsession \ob sesh´ən\ overpreoccupation with an idea, thought or concept

obsessive-compulsive \ob ses´iv—kəm pul´siv\ behavior characterized by ritualistic repetition of certain acts or verbalizations

obstacle sense \ob´stə kəl sens\ ability to avoid unseen objects, usually credited to the blind

obstetrical paralysis \ob stet´ri kəl pə ral´i sis\ paralysis resulting from injury at birth

obstetrics \ob ste´triks\ branch of medicine concerned with pregnancy and childbirth

obturator \ob´´tə rā´ter\ plastic device used to close the opening in a cleft palate so as to improve speech

obtuse \ob´tüs\ being of dull wit or intelligence

occipital \ok sip´i təl\ refers to the back of the head

occipital lobe \ok sip´i təl lōb\ brain lobe located at the occipital extremity

occlusion \ə klü´zhən\ relationship between upper and lower teeth when the mouth is closed

occupational therapy \ok´´yə pā´shə nəl thăr´ə pē\ medically prescribed activity, mental or physical, that is administered by a registered therapist in order to aid in an individual's rehabilitation

ochlesis \ok lē´sis\ physical or mental disorder caused or aggravated by overcrowding

ochlophobia \ok´´lə fō´bē ə\ chronic, unreasonable fear of crowds

octave \ok´təv\ musical tone eight full tones above or below another given note. The lower would have one-half the vibrations of the higher

ocular \ok´yə lėr\ referring to the eye

ocular dominance \ok´yə lėr dom´i nəns\ consistent preference for using the same eye where eye fixation is required

ocular motility \ok´yə lėr mō til´i tē\ eye movement

oculist \ok´yə list\ physician who specializes in treatment of eye disorders

oculistics \ok´´yə lis´tiks\ medical treatment of eye diseases

oculomotor \ok´´yə lō mō´tėr\ relating to eye movements

oculomotor recordings \ok´´yə lō mō´tėr rē kôr´dings\ documentation of eye movement activity

oculopathy \ok´´yə lop´ə thē\ defect or damage of the eye

oculus \ok´yə ləs\ eye

odontic \ō don´tik\ referring to teeth

odynophobia \ō´´ din ə fō´bē ə\ chronic, unreasonable fear of pain

Oedipus complex \ed´ə pəs kom´pleks\ sexual desire of a son for the mother

olfaction \ol fak´shən\ sense of smell

olfactory \ol fak´tə rē\ pertaining to the sense of smell

oligodontia \ol´´i gə don´shə\ less than the normal number of teeth developmentally

oligoencephaly \ol´´i gō en sef´ə lē\ organic mental defectiveness

oligogenic \ol´´i gə jēn´ik\ refers to a hereditary characteristic produced by few genes

oligophrenia \ol´´i gō frē´nē ə\ mental deficiency

oligotrophia \ol´´i gə trō´fē ə\ state of undernutrition

olophonia \ol´´ə fō´nē ə\ speech defect

resulting from malformed organs of speech

omission \ō mish´ ən\ articulatory speech defect in which a sound is omitted

onanism \ō´nə niz´´əm\ the interruption of coitus through penis withdrawal prior to ejaculation

oncology \on kôl´ ə jē\ study of tumors

oncosis \on kō´sis\ condition of developing tumors

oneiric \ō ni´rik\ referring to dreams and their interpretation

oniomania \ō´´nē ə mā´nē ə\ irresistible compulsion to buy things

onychophagia \on´´ə kō fā´jə\ chronic fingernail biting

oocyte \ō´ə sīt´´\ parent cell that develops into an ovum through meiosis

oogenesis \o´´ə jen´i sis\ the process of egg formation through meiosis

ootid \ō´ə tid´´\ ripe ovum derived from the secondary oocyte during oogenesis

open group \ō´pən grüp\ that group open to new members; used to describe either a social or therapeutic group

operant behavior \op´er ənt bė hāv´yėr\ behavior that is maintained or modified by its consequences

operant conditioning \op´ėr ənt kon di´ shə ning\ process used to alter the behavior of human beings and other animals that utilizes the consequences of a behavior to manipulate it

operant level \op´ėr ənt le´vəl\ quantity and quality of observed behavior prior to training or intervention

operator gene \op´ə rā´´tėr jēn\ gene governing the function of one or more genes

ophthalmencephalon \of´´thal men sef´ə lon\ the retina, optic nerve and visual portion of the brain

ophthalmia \of thal´mē ə\ inflammation of the conjuctiva or deeper eye structures

ophthalmia neonatorum \of thal´mē ə nē´´ə nā tör´ əm\ severe conjunctivitis of the newborn

ophtĦalmic \of thal´mik\ ocular; pertaining to the eye

ophthalmitis \of´´thal mī´tis\ inflammation of the eye

ophthalmograph \of thal´mə graf´\ device used to photograph ocular motility while an individual is reading

ophthalmologist \of´´thal mol´ə jist\ physician who specializes in diagnosing and treating diseases of the eye

ophthalmology \of´´thal mol´ə jē\ branch of medicine concerned with diseases and refractive errors of the eye

ophthalmometer \of´´thal mom´ə tėr\ device used to measure the curvature of the cornea

ophthalmoscope \of thal´mə skōp´´\ an instrument designed to illuminate and permit examination of the interior of the eye

opisthotonos \op´´is tho tō´nəs\ spasm characterized by a bowing foward of the body with the head and heels bent backwards

Oppenheim's disease \ōp´en hīmz di sēz´\ amyotonia congenita, congenital general hypotonia of muscles in children

optacon \op´tə kon\ electronic device used by the blind that translates printed material into tactually perceivable vibrations

optic \op´tik\ referring to the eye

optical illusion \op´tik ə lü´zhən\ misperception of visual data

optic atrophy \op´tik a´trə fē\ degeneration of those nerves that communicate between the retina and brain

optic axis \op´tik ak´sis\ central line of vision

optic chiasm \op´tik kī az´əm\ crossing of optic nerve fibers on the undersurface of the brain

optic disk \op´tik disk\ blind spot of the retina

optician \op tish´ən\ expert in the fabrication of lenses and glasses for the correction of refractive errors

optic nerve \op´tik nėrv\ special cell structure that communicates visual information from the retina to the brain

optics \op´tiks\ science of light and its perception

optometrist \op tom´i trist\ expert in the measurement of vision who is licensed to prescribe corrections for refractive errors

oral \ôr´əl\ referring to the mouth or that which is spoken

oral method \ôr´əl meth´əd\ teaching system used with the deaf that involves communication through lip-reading and speech without using sign language

oral reading habit \ôr´əl rē´ding hab´it\ the practice of lip movement while reading to one's self

orb \ôrb\ eye

orbicularis \ôr bik´´yə lâr´is\ refers to muscles that encircle body orifices

orbit \ôr´ bit\ bony socket of the eye

organ \ôr´gən\ specific part of the body that performs a particular function

organic \ôr gan´ik\ pertaining to living organisms

organicity \ôr´´gə nis´i tē\ dysfunction resulting from structural changes

organism \ôr´gə niz´´əm\ individual living entity

organismic age \ôr´gə niz´´mik āj\ individual's age based upon social, educational, mental and skeletal age

organ of Corti \ôr´gən uv kôr´tē\ spiral apparatus in the internal ear

orgasm \ôr´gaz əm\ coital climax

orientation \ôr´´ ē ən tā´shən\ finding one's bearings

orifice \ôr´ə fis\ aperture or opening

orthodontia \ôr´´thə don´shə\ a dental specialty confined to the treatment of malocclusions and teeth irregularities

orthodox \or´thə doks\ that which is generally accepted

orthogenic \ôr´´thə jēn´ik\ refers to treatment aimed at improving mental or psychological functioning

orthography \ôr thog´ rə fē\ art of correct spelling

orthopedic handicap \ôr´´ thə pē´dik

han´dē kap\ physical defect that limits use of body or limbs

orthopedics \ôr´´thə pē´diks\ branch of medicine concerned with the smooth functioning and articulation of the muscular and skeletal systems

orthophoria \ôr´´ thə fôr´ē ə\ normal eye condition in which the visual axes do not deviate from each other when fusion is disrupted

orthopraxia \ôr´´thə prak´sē ə\ medical correction of deformities

orthopsychiatry \ôr´´thō si kī´ə trē\ branch of psychiatry that deals with the normal mental and emotional development of children

orthoptic exercises \ôr thop´tik ek´sėr siz´´ əs\ visual training

orthoptics \ôr thop´tiks\ regimen of eye exercises designed to coordinate the visual axes during binocular vision

oscillation \os´´si lā´shən\ a swinging movement; fluctuation

oscular \os´kyə lėr\ pertaining to the mouth

osmatic \oz ma´tik\ referring to the sense of smell

osseous \os´ē əs\ bony; referring to bones

ossicle \os´i kəl\ small bone

ossification \os´´ə fə kā´shən\ formation of bone, especially the conversion of fibrous tissue, cartilage or membrane into bone

ossify \os´i fī\ to harden into bone

ostectomy \o stek´tə mē\ surgical removal of bone

osteitis \os´´tē i´tis\ inflammation of bone

osteoarthritis \os´´tē ə är thrī tis\ degenerative disease of the joints

osteochondritis \os´´tē ō kon drī´tis\ inflammation of bone and cartilage

osteogenesis \os´´tē ə jen´ə sis\ bone formation

osteology \os´´tē ol´ə jē\ science concerned with bones

osteomalacia \os´´tē ō mə lā´sē ə\ softening of the bone

osteomyelitis \os´´tē ō mī´ə lī´tis\ inflammation of bone

osteopath \os´tē ə path´´\ individual who practices osteopathy

osteopathy \os´´tē op´ə thē\ system of healing that advocates restoration of health through manipulation of bones and muscles while using standard medical methods

osteophone \os´ tē ə fōn\ an instrument used in bone conduction of sound

osteoplasty \os´tē ə plas´´tē\ surgical reconstruction of bone

osteosclerosis \os´´tē ō sklə rō´sis\ abnormal hardening of bone

ostracism \os´trə siz´´əm\ exclusion or banishment from a social group

otitis media \ō tī´tis mē´dē ə\ middle ear infection

otohemineurasthenia \ō´´tō hem´´ə nür´´əs thē´´ nē ə\ nerve deafness in one ear

otologist \ō tol´ə jist\ specialist in the treatment of ears

otology \ō tol´ə jē\ science of ear physiology and disease

otopathy \ō top´ə thē\ damage or disease of the ear

otoplasty \ō´tə plas´´tē\ plastic surgery of the ear

otorhinolaryngology \ō´´tō rī´´ no lǎr´´in gol´ə jē\ the study of the ear, nose and throat and their diseases

otosclerosis \ō´´tə skli rō´sis\ hardening of the ossicles accompanied by a gradual loss of hearing

outpatient \out - pā´shənt\ individual who visits a hospital for diagnosis or treatment but does not become hospitalized

ova \ō´və\ eggs

ovary \ ō´və rē\ female gland that produces eggs

overachievement \ō´vėr ə chēv´mənt\ achievement beyond level expected on basis of intelligence tests

overcompensation \ō´vėr kom´´pen sā´shən\ substitution of excessive positive character traits in an attempt to overcome feelings of inadequacy or inferiority

overlearning \ō´vėr lėr´´ning\ learning by practice beyond the point where further learning can take place or that the degree of learning exceeds its usefulness

overprotection \ō´´vėr prō tek´shən\ care that exceeds normal or judicious limits and thus inhibits the child's (or patient's) ability to cope

overt \ō´vėrt\ objectively observable

ovulate \ō´vyə lāt´´\ to release eggs from the ovary

ovum \ō´vəm\ egg

oxycephalous \ok´´si sef´ə lus\ referring to a head that is pointed and conelike

oxycephaly \ok´´si sef´ə lē\ acrocephaly

oxylalia \ok´´si lal´ē ə\ abnormally rapid speech

ozostomia \ō´´zə stō´mē ə\ malodorous breath; halitosis

P **pacemaker** \pās´mā kėr\ subcutaneous electronic device used to stimulate a normal heartbeat in certain heart conditions

pachydactyly \pak´´ə dak´tə lē\ condition marked by abnormal enlargements of the fingers and toes

pachyglossia \pak´ə glō´rē ə\ abnormal enlargement of the tongue

pachygyria \pak´´ə jē´rē ə\ condition in which the cerebral convolutions are broadened and flattened

pacing \pā´sing\ using electronic devices to regulate the heart; stereotyped walking to and fro that is exhibited by some institutionalized retarded people; matching learning task with developmental level of learner

paired associate learning \părd ə sō´sē ət lėr´ ning\ successive presentation of a list of paired items such as words, pictures, symbols or sounds

palate \pal´ət\ roof of mouth

palatognathous \pal´´ə tog´nə thəs\ possessing a congenital cleft palate

palatoplasty \pal´´ə tō plas´tē\ surgical repair of cleft palate and other palatal defects

palilalia \pal´´i lā´lē ə\ speech aberration characterized by repeating a word or group of words with increasing speed

palingraphia \pal´´in graf´ē ə\ mirror writing

palinlexia \pal´´in leks´ē ə\ reading backward

palliative \pal´i ə tiv\ that which eases pain

pallor \pal´ér\ pale skin condition

palmar response \päl´mər rē spons\ grasping reflex in the newborn

palpable \pal´pə bəl\ detectable to the touch

palpebral \pal´pə brəl\ referring to the eyelids

palpitation \pal´´pi tā´shən\ rapid heartbeat detectable by the patient

palsy \päl´zē\ paralysis

pandemic \pan dem´ik\ describes a disease that is widespread; worldwide

panglossia \pan glos´ē ə\ overtalkativeness due to anxiety

panic \pan´ik\ overwhelming anxiety and fear affecting one's reactions and performance

pannus \pan´nəs\ infiltration of the corneal tissue by new blood vessels; exudate seen in some forms of arthritis, involving the lining of the joint

panogen \pan´ə jen\ methyl mercury quaridine; deadly mercury compound used as a fungicide

panophobia \pan´ə fō´bē ə\ chronic, unreasonable fear of everything; panphobia

panplegia \pan plē´´jē ə\ total paralysis

pantophobia \pan´´tə fō´bē ə\ panophobia or panphobia

papilledema \pap´´əl ə dē´mə\ swelling of the optic nerve head

papule \pap´ūl\ a small bump on the skin

parabiosis \păr´´ə bī ō´sis\ impermanent nerve conduction loss

parachromatopsia \păr´´ə krō´´ mə top´sē ə\ color blindness that is not total in scope

paracusis \păr´´ə kü´sis\ any hearing aberration

parageusia \păr´´ə gü´shə\ taste hallucination

paragrammatism \păr´´ə gram´ə tiz əm\ speech that reveals grammar and syntax difficulties

paragraphia \păr´´ə graf´ē ə\ disorder characterized by inability to spell

parakinesia \păr´´ə ki nē´sē ə\ unnatural bodily movements

paralalia \păr´´ə lā´lē ə\ any speech defect

paralexia \păr´´ə lek´sē ə\ reading defect in which transpositions and substitutions of letters, syllables or words occur

paralipophobia \păr´´ə li pō fō´bē ə\ chronic, unreasonable fear of forgetting or neglecting to do one's duty

parallax \păr´ə laks\ the apparent displacement of an object by a change in the observer's position

parallel play \păr´ə lel plā\ non-cooperative play of children who, though side by side, do not play with each other

paralog \păr´ə log\ nonsense word composed of two syllables

paralogia \păr´´ə lō´jə\ illogical or irrational speech due to mental disorder

paralysis \pə ral´i sis\ impairment of muscle function due to neurological damage

paralysis agitans \pə ral´i sis aj´i tanz´´\ Parkinson's disease

paralytic dementia \păr´´ə lit´ik di men´shə\ paretic dementia; associated with syphilis

parametric \păr´´ə me´trik\ refers to a mathematical constant; measures that have definite limits

paramnesia \păr´´am nē´zhə\ memory defect in which fact and fantasy are confused

paranoia \păr´´ə noi´ə\ mental disorder characterized by systematized delusions of grandeur and/or persecution

paraphasia \păr´´ə fā´sē ə\ form of aphasia characterized by an inability to speak correctly; unintelligible speech; jargon

paraphemia \păr´´ə fē´mē a\ paraphasia

paraphilia \păr´´ə fil´yə\ sexual abnormality

paraphonia \păr´´ə fo´nē ə\ voice abnormality

paraphrasia \păr´´ə frā´zhə\ paraphasia

paraplegia \păr´´ə plē´jē ə\ paralysis of the lower part of the body

parapraxia \păr´´ə prak´sē a\ unpredictable, irrational behavior; motor dysfunction characterized by defect in ability to perform purposeful movements

paraprosexia \păr´´ə prō sek´sē ə\ fixation on certain objects or ideas

parapsia \pə rap´sē ə\ tactual agnosia

parasexuality \păr´´ə sek´´shü al´i tē\ sexual perversion

parasyphilis \păr´´ə sif´ə lis\ disease or condition caused by syphilis

parataxic \păr´´ə tak´sik\ referring to a state of emotional maladjustment

paratype \păr´ə tīp\ influence of the environment on the development of a person or organism; a deviant from a type

parentalism \pə ren´tə liz´´əm\ domination of a child by a parent

paresis \pə rē´sis\ progressive mental defect and paralysis resulting from neurosyphilis; incomplete paralysis

paresthesia \păr´´əs thē´zhə\ abnormal sensation such as numbness, burning or prickling of the skin or body part

parietal lobe \pə rī´i təl lōb\ brain lobe located behind the central sulcus and above the lateral cerebral fissures

parkinsonism \păr´´kin sōn´iz əm\ syndrome characterized by tremors, rigidity, akinesia and loss of voluntary movement; also called Parkinson's disease

parorexia \păr´´ə rek´sē ə\ craving to eat nonfood substances; pica

parosmia \păr os´mē ə\ any problem or disease affecting the sense of smell

paroxia \pə rok´sē ə\ the compulsive ingestion of nonfood items; pica

paroxysm \păr´ok siz´´əm\ sudden outburst of emotion; onset of symptoms

parthenophobia \păr´´thē nə fō´bē ə\ chronic, unreasonable fear of girls

partially hearing \păr´shə lē hēr´ing\ those individuals who can use their hearing to acquire speech and language skills but who may require sound amplification or other special educational services

partially sighted \păr´shə lē sīt´id\ having visual acuity ranging from 20/70 to 20/200 in the better eye after correction

parturition \păr´´tü rish´ən\ process of childbirth

passive \pas´iv\ inactive; exhibiting a lack of participation without desire to exert control in a given situation

passive aggression \pas´iv ə gresh´ən\ signs of submission used by an individual to cover deep feelings of aggression

passive-dependent \pas´iv - di pen´dənt\ reaction characterized by indecision, helplessness and a tendency to rely on others for protection and help

passive hostility \pas´iv hos til´i tē\ characteristic of one who expresses no overt ill will but may refrain from performing friendly or cooperative acts

passive motion \pas´iv mō´shən\ movement of patient's joints carried out by a therapist or an attendant

passiveness \pas´iv nəs\ characteristic of persons who accept external controls with little resistance; submissiveness

Patau's syndrome \pə touz´ sin´drōm\ mental retardation syndrome associated with a trisomy 13 chromosome configuration

patellar reflex \pə tel´ėr rē´fleks\ knee jerk reflex

pathic \path´ik\ referring to disease

pathogen \path´ə jən\ anything that produces disease or damage in an organism

pathogenesis \path´´ō jen´ə sis\ origin of a disease

pathognomonic \pə thog´´nə mon´ik\ characteristic or symptom of a condition that identifies the condition because of its uniqueness

pathognomy \path og´nō mē\ diagnosis or detection of disease

pathological \path´´ə loj´i kəl\ involving or caused by disease

pathology \pə thol´ə jē\ study of the nature of disease, its resulting structural and functional changes

pathomania \path´´ə mā´nē ə\ condition characterized by inability to appreciate, understand or follow the moral or ethical criteria of one's group

pathophobia \path´´ə fō´bē ə\ chronic, unreasonable fear of disease

pathopsychology \path´´ə sī kol´ə jē\ psychology of mental illness

patterning \pat´ėr ning\ a neurophysiological technique used in the reha-

bilitation of brain injured and physically handicapped children

Pavlovian conditioning \pav lō´vē ən kon di´shən ing\ conditioning in which the stimulus precedes the response; classical conditioning

peccatiphobia \pek´´kə tə fō´bē ə\ pathological fear of committing sin

pecking order \pek´ing ôr´dėr\ dominance arrangement among chickens and, by extension, among members of any social group

pectoral \pek tôr´əl\ referring to the chest

pedagogics \ped´´ə goj´iks\ art of teaching; pedagogy

pedagogue \ped´ə gog´\ a school teacher

pedagogy \ped´ə gō´´jē\ teaching

pedal \ped´əl\ referring to the foot

pedantry \ped´ən trē\ excessive display of learning

pederasty \ped´ə ras´´tē\ anal intercourse

pederosis \pē´´dėr ō´sis\ sexual abuse of children

pediatrician \pē´´dē ə trish´ən\ medical doctor specializing in the treatment of children's diseases

pediatrics \pē´´dē ə´triks\ branch of medicine concerned with the care of children

pedigree \ped´ə grē´\ chart illustrating the history of a family with regard to a particular genetic trait

pedologia \ped ə lō´jē ə\ baby talk

pedology \pi dol´ə jē\ the study of child development

pedophilia \pē´´də fil´ē ə\ adult desire for sexual contact with children

pedophobia \pē´´də fō´bē ə\ fear of children

peeper \pē´pėr\ voyeur

peer \pēr\ companion or equal

Pelizaeus-Merzbacher disease \pel´i zā´əs - mėrz bok´ėr di zēz\ hereditary, progressive neurological disease that may result in mental retardation, cerebral palsy and epilepsy

pellagra \pə lā´grə\ nutritional disorder caused by niacin deficiency;

characterized by skin, digestive tract and nervous system dysfunctions

penetrance \pen´i trəns\ regularity with which a gene produces its effect

penile \pē´nīl\ referring to the penis

penilingus \pē´´ni ling´gəs\ fellatio

penis envy \pē´nis en´vē\ in Freudian psychology, the female's covetousness for a penis

penology \pēn o´lō jē\ science that studies criminals and prisons

peptic \pep´tik\ referring to digestion

perceive \pėr sēv´\ to know through the senses

percept \pėr´sept\ thing that is perceived

perception \pėr sep´shən\ conscious recognition of a stimulus

perceptual disorder \pėr sep´chü əl dis ôr´dėr\ condition in which there is an impairment of the integration of auditory, visual or tactile stimuli into awareness

perceptual field \pėr sep´chü əl fēld\ sensory environment available to a perceiving organism

perceptual unity \pėr sep´chü əl ün´i tē\ perception of an object as a unified whole and not as a combination of details or of abstract qualities

performance test \pėr fôr məns test\ nonverbal test

periarthritis \pȧr´´ē ȧrth rī´tis\ inflammation of tissue adjacent to a joint

pericardium \pȧr´´ ə kär´dē əm\ serofibrous sac containing the heart

perimeter \pə rim´i tėr\ instrument that measures the extent of the visual field; border

perinatal \pȧr´´ə nā´təl\ the period shortly before, during and right after the birth process

paripatology \pȧr´´i pə tol´ō jē\ study of environmental mobility, especially with the blind

peripheral \pə rif´ėr əl\ that which is on the boundaries

peripheral dominance \pə rif´ėr əl dom´ə nəns\ functional asymmetry in the use of hand, eye, ear and foot

peripheral nerves \pə rif´ėr əl nėrvz\ nerves of the body emanating from the central nervous system

peripheral vision \pə rif´ėr əl vizh´ən\ discernment of images at the outer edges of the visual field

peristalsis \pȧr ə stol´sis\ alternate constriction and dilation of the digestive tract caused by the action of circular and longitudinal muscles, resulting in propulsive movement of food from the mouth through the alimentary canal

peritoneum \pėr´´i to nē´´əm\ abdominal lining

permissiveness \pėr mis´iv nəs\ an all accepting, laissez faire method of child rearing and discipline

persecution complex \pėr´´sə kū´shən kom´pleks\ condition in which a person feels other people wish to injure or harm him or her

perseveration \pėr´´sev ə rā´shən\ abnormal continuation of an activity

persona \pėr sō´nə\ the mask or front a person presents to the world

personality \pėr´´sə nal´i tē\ total manner in which an individual relates to his environment; includes intellectual, emotional, physical and social characteristics

personality profile \pėr´´sə nal´i tē prō´fīl\ the graphic representation of an individual's personality characteristics

Perthes' hip \pėr´thēz hip\ childhood condition in which the upper end of the femur becomes softened probably due to diminished blood supply

pertussis \pėr tüs´is\ whooping cough

perversion \pėr vėr´zhən\ socially condemned deviation from what is considered normal or proper, especially referent to sexual practices

pervert \pėr´vėrt\ person judged by his own culture as having deviant sexual desires

pes cavus \pes kā´vəs\ pathologically high foot arch

pes planus \pes plā´nəs\ flat feet

pesticide \pes´ti sīd´\ poison used to kill pests

petit mal \pe tē´ mal\ form of epilepsy characterized by brief cessation of activity with falling or overt convulsive activity usually not present

pfropfschizophrenia \fropf´´skit sə frē´nē ə\ mental deficiency accompanied by schizophrenia

phagocyte \fag´ə sīt\ a white cell that attacks foreign bodies in the blood

phagomania \fag´´ə ma´nē ə\ abnormal, insatiable craving for food

phagophobia \fag´´ə fō´bē ə\ fear of eating

phakoma \fə kō´mə\ tiny tumor noted in the retina of tuberous sclerosis patients

phalanges \fə lan´jēz\ plural of phalanx

phalanx \fə lank´s\ any bone of the fingers or toes

phallic \fal´ik\ pertaining to the penis

phallic symbol \fal´ik sim´bəl\ something that resembles a penis

phallus \fal´əs\ a symbol or representation of the penis

phantasm \fan´taz əm\ image of the imagination; fantasm

phantasy \fan´tə sē\ fantasy

phantom limb \fan´təm lim\ persistence of sensation that seems to come from a limb that has been amputated

pharmacology \fär´´mə kol´ə jē\ science of drugs

pharmacomania \fär´´mə kō mā´nē ə\ morbid desire to take unneeded medication

pharmacopeia \fär´´mə kə pē´ə\ an authoritative listing of drugs and medications

pharmacophobia \fär´´mə kō fō´bē ə\ unreasonable fear of taking medications

pharynx \fär´ingks\ tube connecting mouth and esophagus to nasal passages

phenocopy \fē´nō kop´´ē\ environmental replication of a trait that is hereditary in other instances

phenotype \fē´nə tīp´´\ observable characteristics of an organism

phenylalanine \fen´´ə lal´ə nīn\ basic amino acid that occurs naturally in most protein substances

phenylketonuria \fen´´əl kēt´´ə nėr´ē ə\ hereditary defect in which an individual lacks the ability to metabolize a basic amino acid (phenylalanine) with resultant mental retardation

phenylpyruvic acid \fen´´əl pī rüv´ik as´id\ substance excreted in the urine of phenylketonuric individuals as a result of the inability to metabolize phenylalanine

phenylpyruvic oligophrenia \fen´´əl pī rüv´ik ol´´ə gō frē´nē ə\ mental retardation due to phenylketonuria

phlegmatic \fleg mat´ik\ sluggish

phobia \fō´bē ə\ chronic abnormal fear of something such as height, darkness, germs or snakes

phobiac \fō´bi ak\ one who fears

phobophobia \fō´´bō fō´bē ə\ fear of being afraid

phocomelia \fō´´kō mē´ lē a\ congenital defect characterized by abnormal shortening of the limbs due to absence or partial absence of long bones; the hands or feet may be attached to or close to the trunk; this condition has resulted from the use of the drug thalidomide during pregnancy

phonate \fō´nāt\ to speak

phonation \fō nā´shən\ production of vocal sounds

phoneme \fō´nēm\ basic units of sound

phonetics \fə net´iks\ science of sounds of the voice

phonics \fon´iks\ method of teaching reading based upon phonetics

phonogram \fō´nə gram\ written symbol that represents a speech sound

phonology \fə nol´ə jē\ science of vocal sounds

phonopathy \fə nop´ə thē\ disease or defect of speech organs

phonophobia \fō´´nō fō´bē ə\ fear of one's voice

phoria \fôr´ē ə\ any deviation of the eyes from their normal visual axes

photic \fō´tik\ referring to light

photoma \fō tō´mə\ visual hallucination involving flashes of light

photomania \fō''tō mā'nē ə\ psychiatric symptoms induced by stimulation from light

photometer \fō tom'ə tėr\ instrument designed to measure the intensity of light

photo-ophthalmia \fō''tō - ôf thal'mē ə\ eye damage caused by bright light

photophobia \fō''tə fō'bē ə\ abnormal sensitivity to light

photopia \fō tō'pē ə\ vision of strong light as differentiated from night or scotopic vision

phrenoplegia \fren''ə plē'je\ sudden, unexpected attack of mental illness

phthisis \ti'sis\ shrinking or wasting away of a body part

phthisis bulbi \ti'sis bul'bē\ atrophied, sightless eye

physical therapy \fiz'i kəl thär' ə pē\ the use of physical means to treat bodily disorders

physiognomy \fiz''ē og'nə mē\ the face; the study of facial expressions for insight into character, personality or pathological condition

physiology \fiz''ē ol'ə jē\ study of the function of normal diseased body organs

physiopathology \fiz''ē ō pə thol'ə jē\ study of body malfunction due to trauma or disease

physiopsychic \fiz''ē ō sī'kik\ referring to both mental and physical phenomena

physiotherapy \fiz''ē ō thär'ə pē\ treatment of motor dysfunction by physical agents such as heat, massage, and exercise; physical therapy

physique \fiz ēk\ the appearance, structure and organization of a body

pica \pī'kə\ desire to eat nonfood items such as paint, plaster, paper or clay

pickwickian syndrome \pik wik'ē ən sin'drōm\ condition of extreme obesity accompanied by hypoventilation, retention of carbon dioxide and somnolence

Pierre Robin Syndrome \pē ār rōb'ēn sin'drōm\ condition characterized by micrognathia, glossoptosis, cleft palate and possible mental retardation

pigment \pig'mənt\ coloring matter

pilomotor response \pī'lō mō'tər rē spons\ goose bumps

pilosity \pi lōs'i tē \ excessive hairiness

pilot study \pī'lət stud'ē\ small-scale experimentation aimed at ascertaining the feasibility of a larger, more complicated project

pinkeye \pink'ī\ acute, contagious conjunctivitis

pinna \pin'nə\ projected part of the exterior ear

pitch \pich\ the dimension of highness or lowness of a tone

pituitary gland \pi tü'i tăr''ē gland\ gland located at the base of the brain that regulates the functioning of other glands and is important to normal growth and development

PKU \pē kā ū\ abbreviation for phenylketonuria

placebo \plə sē'bō\ inactive preparation that is incapable of producing a medicinal effect but is used to satisfy a patient's desire to be medicated or as a control factor in a scientific study

placenta \plə sen'tə\ an organ attached to the wall of the uterus that connects to the fetus by means of an umbilical cord, possessing a maternal and fetal section; serves to establish biochemical and nutritional communication between mother and fetus

placenta abruptio \plə sen'tə ə brüp'tē ō\ condition in which the placenta is partially separated from the wall of the uterus resulting in decrease of oxygen and nutrition to the fetus

placental dysfunction syndrome \plə sen'təl dis funk'shən sin'drōm\ condition caused by degenerative changes in the placenta that result in progressive reduction of oxygen and nourishment for the fetus

placenta previa \plə sen'tə prē'vē ə\ condition in which the placenta is located low in the uterus so as to interfere with the birth process

plagiocephaly \plā''jē ə sef'ə lē\ head shape characterized by marked asymmetry

planophrasia \plan´´ō frā´zhə\ rapid succession of ideas

planta pedis \plan´tə ped´is\ sole of the foot

plantar crease \plan´tėr krēs\ crease in the skin that runs longitudinally down the sole of the foot from the large toe and the second toe; one of the characteristics of Down's syndrome

plantar reflex \plan´tėr rē´fleks\ automatic response in which the toes flex when the sole of the foot is stimulated

plantigrade \plan´ti grād\ manner of walking in which the entire bottom of the foot touches the ground

plasticity \plas ti´si tē\ ability to modify or be changed

plateau \pla tō´\ a learning period in which little or no observable progress seems to be taking place

platonic \plə ton´ik\ referring to a relationship that is based on friendship and not on sex

platybasia \pla´´tə bā´sē ə\ deformity of the occipital bone in which the foramen magnum is small and misshapen

platycephalic \pla´´ti sə fal´ik\ wideheaded

play therapy \plā thăr´ə pē\ psychotherapeutic technique in which child's use of play materials and fantasy in play is observed and interpreted

pleasure principle \plā´zhür prin´si pəl\ the natural instinct to avoid pain and seek pleasure

pleiotropism \plē´´ō trop´iz əm\ one gene causing apparently different or unrelated effects

pleiotropy \plē ot´rə pē\ the effect of having one gene influence more than one trait

pleniloquence \plə nil´ə kwens\ extreme talkativeness

pleonexia \plē´´ə nek´sē ə\ greediness associated with emotional illness

plexiform \plek´sə form´´\ resembling a network such as nerves or blood-vessels

plexus \pleks´us\ nerve or vein network

plosive \plō´siv\ speech sound made by developing air pressure and suddenly releasing it; examples are p, d and t

plumbism \plum´iz əm\ lead poisoning

plutomania \plü´´tə mā´nē ə\ unhealthy preoccupation with becoming wealthy

pneumoencephalography \nü´´mō en sef´´ə log´rə fē\ science of making x-ray photographs of the brain, usually by injection of gas by lumbar puncture or (rarely) by cisternal puncture

pneumograph \nü´mō graf\ a device that records respiratory function

poise \poiz\ an appearance of ease, composure, dignity and graceful self-assurance

polar body \pō´lėr bo´dē\ small groups of genetic material that migrate from the nucleus of the ovum to its periphery during oogenesis

polioencephalomyelitis \po´lē ō en sef´´ə lō ´´mī´ə lī´tis\ inflammation of the spinal cord and brain due to poliovirus

poliomyelitis \pō´lē ō mī´ə lī´´tis\ viral disease that may result in central nervous system involvement and paralysis; also called infantile paralysis or polio

Pollyanna mechanism \pol ē an´ə mek´ən iz əm\ defense mechanism that distorts reality with an overly optimistic attitude

polyarticular \pol´´ē är tik´yə lėr\ involving many joints

polydactyly \pol´´ē dak´tə le\ congenital defect characterized by additional fingers or toes

polygenic \pol´´ē jen´ik\ influenced or determined by more than one gene

polyglot \pol´ē glot´´\ multilingual; also, a mixture or confusion of different languages

polygraph \pol´e graf\ lie detector; a device for recording changes in bodily reactions

polylogia \pol´´ē lō´jə\ continuous talk; prattle

polymorphism \pol˝ē môr´fiz əm\ existence in a population of alternative common genes; differing blood groups provide a notable example in human beings

polyneuritis \pol˝ē nü rī´tis\ inflammation of the peripheral nerves

polyopia \pol˝ē ō´pē ə\ visual defect in which one object is seen as two or more

polyphagia \pol˝ē fā´jē ə\ excessive desire to eat

polyploidy \pol´ē ploi˝dē\ condition in which there are more than the two full sets of chromosomes in a cell

polyuria \pol˝ē ūr´e ə\ excessive urination

porencephaly \pör˝en sef´ə lē\ condition characterized by cysts or cavities within the brain

porropsia \pôr ōp´sē ə\ visual defect in which objects appear as more distant than they are

posiomania \pō˝sē ə mā´nē ə\ acute alcoholism

positive reinforcement \poz´i tiv rē˝in fôrs´mənt\ process in which a behavior increases in frequency or is strengthened by having the behavior followed by a rewarding consequence

positive reinforcer \poz´i tiv rē˝in fôrs´ėr\ stimulus that follows a response in order to maintain or increase the frequency of the response

postencephalitis \pōst˝en sef˝ ə lī´tis\ describes the condition and behavior of a person after encephalitis

posterior \po stēr´ē ėr\ situated behind or toward the rear

posterior chamber \po stēr´ē ėr chām´bėr\ aqueous space between iris and lens

posthypnotic suggestion \pōst˝hip not´ik sug jest´yən\ a suggestive statement made by a hypnotist during a trance that is carried out unknowingly by the subject upon awakening

postimmunization encephalopathy \pōst im˝yə nī zā´shən en sef˝ə lop´ə thē\ central nervous damage following inoculation with antitetanus serum or vaccines such as small pox, rabies and typhoid

postlingual \pōst ling´gwəl\ after the acquisition of language

postmature \pōst´mə chūr´\ refers to a condition in which the fetus is delivered after a prolonged gestation period

postnatal \pōst nā´təl\ subsequent to birth

post partum \post pär´təm\ temporal period following childbirth

post-test \post´ - test\ a test given after a variable is introduced to measure its effect

posture \pos´chėr\ the way the body is held; an attitude or belief

potency \pō´tən sē\ great or latent power; male sexual capability

potentiality \pə ten˝shē al´ə tē\ refers to what is possible but not yet realized

Pott's disease \pots di zēz´\ tuberculosis of the spine

practice effect \prak´tis ə fekt´\ change in performance brought about by repeating a response or an activity

practice limit \prak´tis lim´it\ point at which practice fails to facilitate performance

praecox \prē´koks\ refers to that which develops early

pragmatic \prag mat´ik\ practical; concern for outcome rather than process

prate \prāt\ to talk foolishly or excessively

preadolescence \prē˝ ad ə les´əns\ period of childhood between nine and twelve years of age

precipitate delivery \prē sip´i tit dī liv´ə rē\ sudden expulsion of the fetus

precision teaching \prē si´zhən tēch´ing\ well planned, specific instruction designed to meet an individual student's needs

precocious \prə kō´shəs\ characterized by rapid early development

preconception \prē˝ kən sep´ shən\ idea formed before consideration of available data

preconscious \prē´kon shus\ referring to memory material that is readily recallable although not presently in mind

predisposition \prē dis´´pə zish´ən\ increased genetically determined probability that a disease or condition may occur under certain environmental circumstances

prefrontal lobotomy \prē front´əl lō bo´tō mē\ brain surgery used to quiet unruly mental patients; no longer popular

pregnancy \preg´nan sē\ the prenatal stages of zygotic, embryonic and fetal development that last approximately 266 days with humans and terminate with childbirth

prehensile \prē hen´sil\ having the ability to grasp

prejudice \pre´jü dis\ prejudgment; a belief based on inadequate data and resistant to change

prelingual \prē ling´gwəl\ before the acquisition of language

prelocomotion \prē´´lō kō mō´shən\ crawling movement prior to ambulation in a young child

prematurity \prē´´mə tér´ə tē\ condition of a child born before prenatal development is completed; sometimes defined as pertaining to all birth weights of less than five and one-half pounds

premorbid personality \prē môr´bid pér´´sə nal´i tē\ behavior characteristics said to be predictive of subsequent disorder

prenatal \pre nā´təl\ before birth

prenubile \prē´nü bil\ pertaining to the span of life prior to puberty

prepotency \prē pō´ten sē\ ability of a genetically determined characteristic to dominate another

prepuberal \prē pü´bér əl\ referring to the one or two years preceding puberty

prerequisite skill \prē rek´wi zit skil\ a skill that must be mastered antecedent to the learning of another skill

presbycusis \pres´´bi kü´sis\ progressive hearing dysfunction due to aging

presbyope \prez´bē ōp´´\ a person with presbyopia

presbyophrenia \pres´´bi ə frē´nē ə\ disorientation, confusion and memory loss associated with advancing age and senility

presbyopia \prez´´bē ō´pē ə\ decreased power of visual accommodation related to increased age and lessened flexibility of the lens of the eye

preschool \prē´skül\ language and social skill training provided for children prior to entering kindergarten; a school that provides such training

prescriptive teaching \prē skrip´tiv tē´ching\ outlining of an individualized educational program for a child

presenile \prē sē´nīl\ condition in which symptoms of senility appear early in life

presenile dementia \prē sē´nīl də men´shə\ early appearance of the type of mental disorders usually associated with advanced age; Alzheimer's disease

pressure sensation \presh´ér sen sā´shən\ the body's sense modality that registers the exertion of force against the skin or other organ

pretest \prē´test\ test given before a variable is introduced in order to determine the baseline

prevalence \prev´ə lənts\ number of cases of a particular disease or condition within a specified area at a given time

prevocational \prē´´ vō kā´shən əl\ refers to training preparatory to entering a vocational training program

prezygotic \prē´´zi got´ik\ occurring prior to conception

priapism \prī´ə piz əm\ chronic penis erection without accompanying sexual desire

primacy \prī´mə sē\ state of being first

primal \prī´məl\ occurring first

primary \prī´măr ē\ first in rank

primary amentia \prī´măr ē ā men´shə\ mental defect caused by inheritance

primipara \prī mip´ér ə\ female who has produced offspring one time

primordium \prī môr´dē əm\ a rudimentary part during development

privation \prī vā´shən\ lack

probability \prob´´ə bil´i tē\ likelihood of an event's taking place

probable \prob´ə bəl\ likely

proband \prō´band\ first person in a family tree with a certain characteristic or disorder evident; also called propositus

probation \prō bā´shən\ a trial period of conditional release

problem solving \prob´ləm sol´ving\ selection process of choosing correct alternative that will lead to desired goal

procedure \prō sē´ jèr\ way of conducting an experiment

procreation \prō´´krē ā´shən\ sexual reproduction

prodigy \prod´i jē\ a child who exhibits an exceptional talent early in life

prodromal \prō drōm´əl\ symptom that forecasts the approach of a disease; prodromic

productivity \prō´´duk tiv´i tē\ amount of work produced or accomplished

proficiency \prō fish´ən sē\ capability; competence

progenitor \prō jen´ i tèr\ ancestor in whom a condition or characteristic originates genetically

progeny \proj´ə nē\ offspring

progeria \prō jèr´ē ə\ premature old age

prognathism \prog´nə thiz´´əm\ marked projection of the upper or lower jaw

prognosis \prog nō´sis\ prediction of outcome of a disease or disease process

projection \prə jek´shən\ the psychological process of assigning to others one's own wishes, traits or behaviors

projective technique \prə jek´tiv tek nēk´\ method used in testing designed to determine personality characteristics; individual required to ascribe own feelings and thoughts to a relatively ambiguous stimulus

prolonged delivery \prō longd´ di liv´ə rē\ labor extended beyond usual time limits

pronation \prō nā´shən\ act of turning the palm of the hand downward

propagation \prop´´ə gā´shən\ reproduction

propensity \prō pen´si tē\ inclination

prophase \prō´fāz\ first phase of cell division characterized by the transformation of the irregular network of chromatin material of the interphase nucleus into spirally coiled threads that then become doubled, shortened and thickened to form individual chromosomes; this phase terminates with the disappearance of the nuclear membranes, at which point metaphase begins

prophylaxis \prō´´fə lak´sis\ disease prevention

propositus \prə poz´i təs\ proband

proprioceptor \prō´´prē ə sep´tèr\ refers to an organ sensitive to position and movement of the body

prosopoplegia \prō´´sə pō plē´jə\ paralysis of the face

prosthesis \pros thē´sis\ an artifical body part or limb

prosthodontics \pros´´thə don´tiks\ branch of dentistry dealing with construction of artificial appliances for the mouth or teeth

protanomaly \prō´´tə nom´ə lē\ visual insensitivity to red portion of the spectrum

protanopia \prō´´tə nō´prē ə\ red color blindness

protein-calorie malnutrition \prō´ tēn-kal´ə rē mal´´nü trish´ən\ reduction of essential food intake during critical growth period that may result in mental and physical disability

prototype \prō´tə tīp\ earlier or earliest form

proximal \prok´si məl\ point of a body part nearest the midline

pseudodementia \sü´´dō də men´shə\ temporary social and intellectual incompetence due to emotional distress

pseudofeeblemindedness \sü´dō

fē´´bəl mīn´did nəs\ older term for pseudo mental retardation

pseudohypertrophic \sü´´dō hī´´pėr trō´fik\ refers to a form of muscular dystrophy characterized by apparent increase in muscle size with loss of strength and motor control

pseudohypertrophy \sü´´dō hī pėr´trə fē\ increase of size with loss of function

pseudoisochromatic \sü´´dō ī´´ sə krō ma´tik\ refers to using differing colors to detect color blindness

pseudomemory \sü´´dō mem´ėr ē\ false recall of something not experienced

pseudo mental retardation \sü´dō men´təl rē´´tär dā´shən\ retardation due to social, psychological or other causes rather than organic causes

pseudoplegia \sü´´dō plē´jē ə\ paralysis due to hysteria

psychalgia \si kal´jə\ physical pain of psychological origin; hysterical pain

psyche \sī´kē\ the human spirit, mind or self; soul

psychiatric social worker \sī kē at´rik sō´shəl wėr´kėr\ one trained to work with mental illness in families

psychiatrist \si kī´ə trist\ physician specializing in the treatment and prevention of mental illness

psychiatry \si kī´ə trē\ that branch of medicine concerned with disorders to the mind

psychic activity \sī´kik ak tiv´i tē\ mental activity

psychic trauma \sī´kik trä´mə\ an experience that produces damage to the psyche

psychoactive \sī´´kō ak´tiv\ capable of influencing psychological status or behavior

psychoanalysis \sī´´kō ə nal´i sis\ Freudian term referring to the use of interviews, free association, dream analysis and interpretation of an individual's reactions to daily events in a therapeutic process

psychodiagnosis \sī´´kō dī´´əg nō´sis\ determination of a disease or condition through the use of psychological tests

psychodrama \sī´´kō drä´mə\ group therapy technique in which patients dramatize their problems

psychoeducational \sī´´kō ed´´jü kā´shən əl\ refers to evaluations and programs that are concerned with both educational and psychological treatment

psychogenetics \sī´´kō jə ne´tiks\ study of the inheritance of psychological traits

psychogenic \sī´´kō jen´ik\ having a psychological origin

psychognosis \sī kog´nō sis\ complete study of a person's mental functioning

psycholinguistics \sī´´kō ling gwis´tiks\ study of the interaction between language and behavior

psychologist \sī kol´ə jist\ expert in psychology

psychology \sī kol´ə jē\ branch of science concerned with behavior; study of the mind

psychometrics \sī´´kō me´triks\ measurement and evaluation of intelligence and other aspects of behavior through psychological testing

psychometry \sī kom´ə trē\ measurement of psychological variables, such as intelligence, behavior, attitude and emotional reactions

psychomotor \sī´´kō mō´tėr\ physical effects of mental activity

psychomotor epilepsy \sī´´kō mō´tėr ep´ə lep´´sē\ type of epilepsy usually associated with temporal lobe pathology; seizures are characterized by purposeful but inappropriate motor behavior

psychoneurosis \sī´´kō nü rō´sis\ disorder that is psychogenic in origin

psychopath \sī´kə path´´\ person whose actions persistently violate legal and social mores and whose behavior is directed toward gratification of own needs without regard for the needs of others

psychopathology \sī´´kō pə thol´ə jē\ systematic study of mental disorders in terms of etiology, characteristics and processes

psychopathy \sī kop´ə thē\ disorder of the mind and thought processes

psychopedics \sī´´kō pē´diks\ psychological treatment of children

psychopharmacology \sī´´kō fär´´mə kol´ō ge\ study of the effects of drugs on the psychological functions of the individual

psychosexual \sī´´kō sek´shü əl\ referring to the mental or emotional aspect of sexual drive

psychosis \sī kō´sis\ complex mental disorder characterized by loss of contact with reality

psychosocial \sī´´kō sōsh´əl\ pertaining to the psychological effects of the social environment

psychosomatic \sī´´kō sō mat´ik\ physical disorder that is caused or related to the emotional state of the patient

psychosurgery \sī´´kō sėr´jə rē\ treatment of mental illness by brain surgery

psychotherapy \sī´´ko thăr´ə pē\ behavioral treatment of mental disorder

psychotic \sī kot´ik\ describing behavior associated with psychosis

psychotropic drugs \sī´´kō trō´pik drugz\ medicine or narcotics that affect mental activity

ptosis \tō´sis\ drooping upper eyelid

pubertas praecox \pū´bėr təs prē´koks\ reaching puberty at an early age

puberty \pū´bėr tē\ period of life when the reproductive organs mature

pubescent \pū bes´ənt\ entering puberty

puerilism \pü´ėr ə liz´´ əm\ condition in which an adult regresses to a childlike state

puerperal \pü ėr´pər əl\ referring to parturition

pulmonary \pul´mə năr´´ē\ referring to the lungs

punishment \pun´ish mənt\ in behavioristic terms, refers to the presentation of a negative stimulus or the removal of a positive stimulus in order to extinguish a response

punitiveness \pū´ni tiv´´nəs\ act of inflicting excessive punishment

pupil \pū´pəl\ opening in the center of the iris that permits light rays to enter the eye

pupillary \pū´pi lăr´´ē\ referring to students; referring to the pupil of the eye

pupillary reflex \pū´pil lăr´´ē rē´fleks\ automatic size change in the pupil for light or distance accommodation

pyknic \pik´nik\ body type characterized by well-rounded external contours

pyknolepsy \pik´nə lep´´sē\ form of petit mal epilepsy characterized by a high frequency of seizure activity

pyogenic \pī´ə jen´´ik\ pus producing

pyrexia \pī rek´sē ə\ feverish condition

pyrogenic \pī´´rə jen´ik\ fever producing

pyromania \pī´´rə mā´nē ə\ compulsion to start fires

pyrophobia \pī´´rə fō´bē ə\ irrational fear of fire

pyrosis \pī rō´sis\ heartburn

Q **quack** \kwak\ a person who purposely misrepresents his skills, training or experience in a professional capacity

quadrantanopia \kwod´´rant ə nō´pē ə\ visual defect affecting 25 percent of the visual field

quadriplegia \kwod´´rə plē´jē ə\ paralysis of all four extremities

qualitative \kwol´i tā tiv\ pertains to quality or qualities

quantitative \kwon´´ti tā´ tiv\ refers to describing or measuring of a quantity

quarantine \kwor´ən tēn\ restriction of movement or passage as a means of restricting the spread of communicable disease

questionnaire \kwes´´chə nãr\ list of questions to be utilized for statistical analysis

quickening \kwik´ə ning\ the first detectable fetal movement

quicksilver \kwik´sil´vėr\ mercury

quotidian \kwō tid´ē ən\ fever, seizure or attack that occurs on a daily basis; used in referring to a type of malaria

R **race** \rās\ ethnic subdivision of mankind

rachioparalysis \ra˝kē ō pə ral´i sis\ paralysis of the spinal musculature

rachioplegia \ra˝kē ō plē´jə\ rachioparalysis

rachioscoliosis \ra˝kē ō skō˝lē ō´sis\ condition characterized by lateral curvature of the spine

rachischisis \rak˝i ski´sis\ congenital fissure in the spinal column

radiation \rā˝dē a´shən\ emission of atomic particles

radical \rad´i kəl\ favoring basic, rapid change

radioactive \rā˝dē ō ak´tiv\ quality of emitting atomic particles

radiograph \rā´dē ō graf´\ x-ray picture

radioisotope \rā˝dē ō ī´sə tōp´\ isotope of an element that emits charged particles

radiology \rā˝dē ol´ə jē\ the science of using x-ray photographs for medical diagnosis; also of using radiation for treatment

rage \rāj\ extreme, violent anger

random \ran´dum\ that which occurs by chance or without active intervention

random sample \ran´dum sam´pəl\ chance selection of items to be used in a scientific experiment

range \rānj\ area between the upper and lower limits of a series of values; used in such terms as I.Q range or the mild range of mental retardation

rapport \ra pôr´\ relationship of ease, harmony and accord between the subject and examiner or therapist

ratiocination \rash˝ē os˝ə nā´shən\ process of reasoning or thinking logically

rationalization \rash˝ə nəl ī za´shən\ defense mechanism through which an individual attempts to justify his or her behavior

reaction \rē ak´shən\ response to stimulation

reaction formation \rē ak´shən fôr mā´shən\ defense mechanism in which an ego-threatening impulse is covered over or converted into behavior that expresses the contrary

reactive disorder \rē ak´tiv dis ôr´dér\ behavior disorder caused by reaction to environmental stress

reading disability \rēd´ing dis˝ə bil´i tē\ dyslexia

realistic goals \rē˝ə lis´tik gōlz\ objectives to be sought by an individual that can be achieved by reason of his or her background, education, emotionality and reason

reality adaptation \rē al´i tē ə dap tā´shən\ ability to interpret accurately the external environment in relation to self

reality therapy \rē al´i tē thăr´ə pē\ treatment emphasis upon assisting the patient to cope with his own environment as opposed to treatment in a special milieu

recall \rē´kôl\ the process of remembering stored items

receptive aphasia \rē sep´tiv ə fā´zhə\ disturbance of speech due to brain lesion in which the major difficulty is inability to comprehend the meaning of words and other sounds; also auditory aphasia

receptivity \rē˝sep tiv´i tē\ ability to receive or to be influenced

receptor \rē sep´tér\ specially designed organ that receives sensations

recessive \rē ses´iv\ in genetics, the term refers to those characteristics that can only be expressed when carried by genes from both parents

recessive gene \ rē ses´iv jēn\ a gene that fails to produce its effect in the presence of a contrasting gene ·

recessive tendency \rē ses´iv ten´dən sē\ tendency to withdraw from society

recidivation \re˝sid i vā´shən\ return of a disease or condition; relapse

recidivism \rē sid´ə viz˝əm\ recurrence of antisocial behavior despite treatment or punishment; return to institutionalization

reciprocal movement \rē sip´rə kəl mūv´mənt\ movement of both arms and/or both legs at the same time but in opposite directions

recognition \re kəg ni´shən\ a form of learning in which familiar items are recognized

recollection \rek ə lek´shən\ recalling

recombination \rē kom´bə nā´´shən\ rearrangement of linked genes due to exchange of homologous segments of chromosomes

recon \rē´kon\ smallest part of genetic material that is interchangeable but cannot be fragmented by recombination

recreation \rek rē ā´shən\ play; refreshing activity

reductional division \rē duk´shən əl di vi´shən\ first miotic division characterized by the mere separation of members of homologous pairs of chromosomes, resulting in a reduction in the chromosome number from the somatic or diploid number to the haploid number

referral \rē fėr´əl\ the process of recommending a client or patient for professional service

reflex \rē´fleks\ involuntary movement response to a stimulus

refraction \rē frak´shən\ deviation of light from one medium to another of differing density; specifically refers to the process of correcting visual defects with anteocular lenses

refractive error \rē frak´tiv ăr´ėr\ inability of light rays to be brought to a single focus on the retina due to a structural defect in the eye

refracture \rē frak´chėr\ to break a bone that has previously been broken and healed poorly in order to effect correct union

regimen \rej´i mən\ precise regulation of medication, diet, exercise or practice

regression \rē gresh´ən\ return to a less mature or earlier form of behavior

regulator gene \reg´´yə lā´tėr jēn\ gene that represses the function of an operator gene

regurgitation \rē gėr´´ji tā´shən\ return of solids or fluids to the mouth from the stomach; vomiting

rehabilitation \rē´´ə bil´´i tā´shən\ treatment and training designed toward the attainment of the individual's maximal potential for normal living from the physical, psychological, economic, social and vocational standpoint

reinforcement \rē´´in fôrs´mənt\ presentation of a reward in order to increase the frequency of a response

reintegration \rē´´in tə grā´shən\ return to normal psychiatric functioning after a period of dysfunction

rejection \rē jek´shən\ process of withholding normal recognition, affection or contact

relapse \rē laps´\ return of illness or pathological condition

relationship \rē lā´shən ship´´\ connection or influence; belonging to the same family

relaxation \rē´´lak sā´shən\ opposite of contraction; return to normal; period of rest

relearning \rē lėrn´ing\ learning again what has been learned in the past and forgotten

reliability \rē lī´´ə bil´i tē\ accuracy with which a test measures a trait

remedial \rə mē´dē əl\ serving to improve in function that which is lacking

remedial reading \rə mē´dē əl rē´ding\ techniques used to improve reading ability

remedial teaching \rə mē´dē əl tē´ching\ instruction that is designed to strengthen areas of academic weakness

remission \rē mish´ən\ reduction or disappearance of symptoms

renal \rēn´əl\ referring to the kidneys

replication \rep´´li kā´shən\ the repeat of an experiment for verification of previous experimental results

representative sample \rep´´rē zen´tə tiv sam´pəl\ a selection that represents or truly characterizes the entire population

repression \rē presh´ən\ shutting off

from conscious awareness painful thoughts or memories

reproduction \rē´´prə duk´shən\ the process that culminates in the union of sperm and egg; propagation

repulsion \rē pul´shən\ feeling of aversion

resentment \rē zent´mənt\ indignation

reserve \rē zėrv´\ tendency to hold back or stand off

residual \rē zij´ū əl\ remaining

residual hearing \rē sij´ū əl hēr´ing\ auditory acuity that remains following disease or trauma of the hearing apparatus

resignation \rez´´ig nā´shən\ giving up

resistance \rē zis´təns\ natural ability to stave off debilitating effects of microorganisms, toxic agents etc.; disinclination to recall repressed memories

resonance \rez´ə nəns\ sound quality of the voice due to the size, shape and texture of the vocal tract

resource room \rē´sôrs rüm\ classroom used for special training purposes, usually across categories

respiration \res´´pə rā´shən\ act of breathing

respiratory \res´pėr ə tôr´ē\ referring to breathing or the breathing organs

respirograph \rə spī´rə graf\ record of breathing patterns

respite care \res´´pit kăr\ temporary placement of handicapped child in an institution or foster home in order to provide parents with a relief or vacation time

respondent behavior \rē spon´dənt bē hāv´yėr\ reflexive response; response elicited by a stimulus

response \rē spons´\ reaction to stimulus

responsiveness \rə spon´siv nəs\ ability to react appropriately to others

retard \rē tärd´\ to hold back or delay as in development, growth or achievement

retardate \rē tär´dāt\ mentally retarded individual

retardation \rē´´tär dā´shən\ delayed or subaverage mental or physical growth

retention \rē ten´shən\ memory; process of remembering

retentiveness \rē ten´tiv nəs\ facility in retention

reticular \ri tik´yə lėr\ having a netlike formation

retina \ret´ə nə\ expansion of optic nerve that forms the light receptive structure of the eye

retinal detachment \ret´ə nəl dē tach´mənt\ separation of the retina from the choroid

retinitis \ret´´ə nī´tis\ inflammation of the retina

retinitis pigmentosa \ret´´ə nī´tis pig´´men tō´sə \ chronic degenerative disease of the retina

retinoblastoma \ret´´ə nō blas tō´mə\ malignant intraocular tumor that is most commonly noted in young children

retinography \re´´ti nog´rə fē\ retinal photography

retinopathy \re´´tə nop´ə thē\ disease or abnormal development of the retina

retinoscope \ret´´ə nōs´kōp\ instrument used to help determine the refractive status of the eye

retroactive \re trō ak´tiv\ referring to the past or to a backward direction

retroflex \re trō´ fleks\ referring to being bent backwards

retrograde \re trō´grād\ going backwards

retrography \re trog´rə fē\ mirror writing

retrolental fibroplasia \re´´trō len´təl fī´´brō plā´ zhə\ blindness caused by a dense fibrous growth behind lens of the eye believed to be associated with high concentration of oxygen in incubators where baby was kept in early months of life

reversion \rē vėr´zhən\ reappearance of a genetic trait that has not appeared for several generations or of a psychological stage that had been outgrown

reward \ri wôrd´\ a reinforcing stimulus or object

rhabdophobia \rab´´də fō´bē ə\ abnormal fear of being beaten or otherwise physically punished

rhagades \rag´ə dēz\ cracks in the skin

rheumatic fever \rü mat´ik fē´vėr\ multisystem disease considered to be a complication of streptococcal infection of the upper respiratory tract; acute manifestations may include fever, arthritis, chorea, heart inflammation, characteristic rash and skin nodules

rheumatism \rü´mə tiz´´əm\ a condition characterized by inflammation of the joints and connective tissues

rheumatoid arthritis \rü´mə toid´´ ärth rī´tis\ systemic disease whose cause is unknown; damage to joints an important feature of the disease

Rh factor \är´āch fak´tėr\ Rhesus factor, a substance found in the blood of about 85 percent of Caucasians who are therefore termed Rh+; those whose blood lacks the substance are termed Rh−

Rh incompatibility \är´āch in´´kom pat ə bil´i tē\ situation in which a mother has Rh negative blood and her fetus has Rh positive blood, thus creating a potential for antibody formation in the mother; maternal antibodies may attack Rh+ red blood cells in subsequent pregnancies causing mental retardation or fetal deaths

rhinitis \rī nī´tis\ inflammation of nose lining

rhinolalia \rī´´nō lā´lē ə\ nasal quality of speech due to defect or disease of the nasal passageways

rhythmicity \rith mis´i tē\ degree of regularity manifested by biological functions, such as sleep or toilet activity

rickets \rik´´its\ crippling childhood disorder caused by a deficiency of vitamin D; there are also vitamin D resistant forms of rickets

riddance reflex \rid´əns rē´fleks\ one that removes the organism from contact with a painful stimulus

rigidity \ri jid´ə tē\ form of paralysis in which extensors and flexors contract simultaneously, thus limiting motion

rivalry \rī´vəl rē\ struggle to outdo another

RNA \är en ā\ ribonucleic acid; nucleic acid that transmits coding for specific cellular functions

Rochester method \rä´ches tėr meth´əd\ teaching method of total communication for the deaf that uses both oral and manual techniques

rods \rodz\ cell structures within the eye that specialize in detecting motion and night vision

roentgen \rent´jən\ standard unit of radiation

roentgenism \rent´´jə niz´´əm\ illness or pathology caused by exposure to radiation

roentgenology \rent´´jə nol´ō jē\ science dealing with the use of X rays in medical diagnosis and therapy

roentgenotherapy \rent´´jə nō thăr´ə pē\ use of X rays in treatment of disease

role \rōl\ behavior exhibited by an individual in order to create a desired effect upon observers and fulfill their expectations of him or her; the part or parts one plays in life

role conflict \rōl´ kon´flikt\ disharmony created by contradictory expectations from two or more roles

Romberg's sign \rom´bėrgz sīn\ condition in which swaying and/or falling results from standing with feet together and eyes shut; also known as Romberg's symptom

rooting reflex \rüt´ing rē´fleks\ a baby's automatic response to having its cheek stroked: it turns its head, opens its mouth

rote learning \rōt´ lėrn´ing\ memorization

rubella \rü bel´ə\ viral disease accompanied by a rash and fever; also called German measles

rubeola \rü´bē ō´la\ measles

Rubinstein-Taybi syndrome \rü´´ ben stīn´ tā´bē sin´drōm\ condition characterized by microcephaly, visual defects, abnormally broad thumbs and toes, short stature and mental retardation

S | **Sabin's vaccine** \sā´binz vak´sēn\ oral antipolio vaccine, effective against the three polio strains

saccadic movement \ sə kād´ik müv´mənt\ rapid eye movement from one point to another as in reading

Sach's disease \saks di zēz´\ Tay-Sachs disease

sacral \sāk´rəl\ referring to the sacrum

sacrum \sak´rum\part of the backbone that contributes to forming the pelvis

sadism \sad´iz əm\ deviation characterized by sexual gratification through inflicting pain upon others

sadomasochistic \sā´´dō mas´´ə kis´tik\ evidencing both sadistic and masochistic impulses

sagittal suture \saj´i təl sü´chėr\ one of the cranial sutures; if closed prematurely, a cranial defect known as scaphocephaly may result

Saint Vitus' dance \sānt vī´təs dans\ Syndenham's chorea; a form of chorea distinct from acute chorea

salaam seizure \sə lom´ sē´zhėr\ akinetic seizure

saliva \sə lī´və\ a moistening secretion of the salivary glands that contains ptyalin, the digestive enzyme in the mouth

salivary \sal´i văr ē\ referring to saliva

Salk vaccine \ salk vak´sēn\ vaccine given by injection that protects against the three poliomyelitis viruses

salpingectomy \sal´´pin jek´tə mē\ surgical tying or cutting of the Fallopian tubes so that no eggs can descend to be fertilized; a form of contraception

saltation \sal tā´shən\ a mutation; leaping

saltatory \sal´tə tôr ē\ referring to dance; making abrupt movements forward, such as leaps in progress or transition

salubrious \sə lü´brē əs\ healthful; promoting good health

sample \sam´pəl\ representative number of items selected from a given population; to take a sample

sanction \sank´shən\ permission or approval

sanity \san´i tē\ soundness of mental health

sapid \sap´id\ having taste or flavor

sapphism \saf´iz əm\ lesbianism

sarcasm \ sär´kaz əm\ ridicule; irony

sarcoma \sär kō´mə\ malignant tumor of connective tissue

satiation \sā´´shē ā´shən\ process in which full gratification of a desire is encouraged to the point where the behavior involved is extinguished

saturation \sach´´ə rā´shən\ state of being full or soaked

saturnism \sat´´ėrn iz´əm\ lead poisoning, plumbism

satyr \sā´tėr\ man afflicted with satyriasis

satyriasis \sat´ə rī´ə sis\ abnormally strong sexual drive in a male

scapegoat \skāp´gōt\ one on whom aggression and blame are displaced

scaphocephalic \ska´´fō sə fal´ik\ having a deformed, long head

scaphocephaly \ska´´fō sef´ ə lē\ a form of craniostenosis characterized by a long, narrow, boat-shaped head, usually associated with premature closure of sagittal sutures

scatological \skat´´ə loj´i kəl\ referring to feces; obscene

scatophagy \skə tof´ə jē\ eating of feces

scatophilia \skat´´ə fil´ē ə\ preoccupation with feces

schism \siz´əm\ separation into disharmonious parts

schismogenesis \siz´mō jen´ə sis\ making of a schism or breach

schizoid \skit´soid\ personality type characterized by withdrawn, unsocial, introspective behavior

schizophasia \skit´´sə fā´zhə\ muttered, incomprehensive speech of the schizophrenic

schizophrenia \skit´´sə frē´nē ə\ group of mental disorders marked by disturbances in reality, perception and relationships

schizoprosopia \skit´´sə prə sō´pē ə\ facial fissure as in harelip

schizothymia \skit´´zō thī´mē ə\ schizoidlike behavior within the bounds of normalcy; schizothemia

Scholz's disease \shōlts´əz di zēz´\ juvenile metachromatic leukodystrophy

school phobia \skül fō´bē ə\ chronic, irrational fear of attending school that may be accompanied by somatic complaints such as dizziness, nausea, rash or abdominal pain

scissor gait \siz´ér gāt\ gait characterized by one foot being passed in front of the other due to spasticity of the abductor muscles of the thigh

sclera \sklăr´ə\ white outer coat of the eye

scleritis \sklə rī´tis\ inflammation of the sclera

sclerosis \sklə rō´sis\ hardening of tissue from a disease process

sclerotic coat \skli rot´ik cōt\ outer covering of the eyeball

scoliosis \skō´´lē ō´sis\ lateral curvature of the spine

scopophilia \skō´´pə fil´ē ə\ voyeurism

scoterythrous \skō´´tə rith´rəs\ color vision deficiency in which the red end of the spectrum is darkened

scotoma \skō tō´mə\ area of reduced vision or blindness within the visual field

scotophilia \skō´´tə fil´ē ə\ strong attraction for darkness

scotophobia \skō´´tə fō´bē ə\ chronic, unreasonable fear of darkness

scotopia \skō tō´pē ə\ night vision; vision of dim light

screen \skrēn\ psychologial mechanism that conceals reality in symbols, as in dreams

screening \skrēn´ing\ the use of brief test procedures with large groups in order to locate candidates for more detailed examination

scurvy \skér´vē\ nutritional disorder caused by vitamin C deficiency

sebastomania \sə bas´´tə mā´nē ə\ mental disorder characterized by over-preoccupation with religion

secondary amentia \sek´´ən dăr´ē ə men´shə\ mental defect caused by external factors

secondary drives \sek´´ən dăr´ē drīvz\ motivations for such things as prestige, wealth or religion that may be present in most people but absent from animals and the profoundly retarded

secondary reinforcer \sek´´ən dăr´ē rē´´in fôrs´ér\ a stimulus that acquires strength by being paired with a primary reinforcer

secondary sex characteristic \sek´´ən dăr´ē seks kăr´´ək tér is´tik\ physical characteristic that develops during puberty as the result of sexual maturation

secretion \sə krē´shən\ the development of a biochemical substance by a gland; the substance produced by a gland

sedation \sə dā´shən\ calming or reduction of activity through drugs

sedative \sed´ə tiv\ a drug that calms or lowers the activity of a patient

segregation \seg´´rə gā´shən\ selective separation of differing population subgroups; in genetics, refers to the separation of genes during gametogenesis

seizure \sē´zhér\ epileptic attack

selection \sə lek´shən\ preference of one genotype over another due to greater fitness

self \self\ identity or essential qualities of any person or thing

self-awareness \self-ə wăr´nəs\ being able to identify one's own particular qualities of behavior or thoughts

self-concept \self-kon´sept\ the way a person sees himself

self-destructive behavior \self-dē struk´tiv bē hāv´yer\ self-mutilation; most common forms among the retarded are head banging, biting, slapping and tearing at body orifices

self-fulfilling prophecy \self-ful fil´ing pro´fə sē\ tendency of expectations to influence the outcome of events

self-image \self-im´əj\ the mental picture a person has of himself

self-preservation \self-prez´´ér vā´shən\ activities performed to maintain one's life

self-realizaton \self-rē´´ə lī zā´shən\ actualizing of one's potential

self-reliance \self-rē lī´əns\ tendency to trust one's own judgment

self-righteousness \self-rīt´chəs nəs\ excessive need to appear more moral and well intentioned than others

self-stimulation \self-stim´´yə lā´shən\ phenomenon in which an individual initiates repetitive, stereotyped activity in order to elicit sensory feedback

semantic \sə man´tik\ referring to the meaning of words

semeiology \sē´´mi ol´ə jē\ study of signs and symptoms

semen \sē´men\ fluid containing spermatozoa

semicircular canals \sem´´ē sėr´ku lėr kə nalz´\ the part of the inner ear that functions to maintain balance and equilibrium

semiplegia \sem´´i plē´jə\ hemiplegia

senescence \sə nes´əns\ the aging process

senility \sə nil´i tē\ physical and mental weakness associated with advanced age

sensation \sen sā´shən\ feeling produced by stimulation of the sense organs

sense organ \sens ôr´gən\ any bodily organ designed to receive sensations

sensor \sens´ėr\ a sense receptor

sensorimotor \sen´´sə rē mō´tėr\ pertaining to the pathway from sensor to muscle

sensorineural hearing loss \sen´´sə rē nėr´əl hēr´ing los\ nerve deafness; hearing loss caused by inner ear or neurological pathology

sensorium \sen sôr´ē əm\ parts of the body that deal with sensation

sensory \sen´sə rē\ pertaining to sensation

sensory defects \sen´sə rē dē´feks\ any defect of the senses; usually refers to deficits of hearing and vision

sensory deprivation \sen´sə rē dep´´rə vā´shən\ prolonged reduction or absence of sensory stimulation; principally visual or auditory

sensory discrimination \sen´sə rē dis krim´´ə nā´shən\ ability to respond to differences in sensation

sensory motor \ sen´sə rē mō´tėr\ relating to the interaction of sensation and movement; sensorimotor

separation anxiety \sep´´ə rā´shən ang zī´ə tē\ fear and worry induced by anticipation of, or actual separation from, a loved one

septum \sep´tum\ dividing wall between cavities in the body

sequela \sə kwē´lə\ residual of a disease or accident

sequestration \sē´´kwes trā´shən\ the isolation of a student or patient for training or treatment purposes

serology \sə rol´ə jē\ science dealing with serums

serum \sēr´əm\ fluid that discharges from coagulated blood, used extensively in diagnosis

shock \shok\ reduced vital functioning of the body after trauma which, if untreated, can result in death

shoreline \shôr´līn\ any physical structure that serves as a substantial landmark for the blind, such as a wall, sidewalk or curbing

shunt \shunt\ surgical device used to treat hydrocephalus

sib \sib\ sibling

sibilant \sib´i lənt\ high frequency speech sounds as produced by ch, j, s and z

sibling \sib´ling\ brother or sister

sibling rivalry \sib´ling rī´vəl rē\ competition for attention and affection between siblings

sibship \sib´ship\ relationship between persons born to the same parents

sickle cell anemia \sik´əl sel ə nē´mē ə\ hereditary blood cell defect found chiefly among blacks that causes anemia, organ dysfunction, crippling and death

sicklemia \sik´´ə lē´mē ə\ sickle cell disease

side effect \sīd ə fekt´\ other than desired results from drugs, medications or treatments

sight \sīt\ the visual faculty

sign \sīn\ evidence of disease that can

be objectively perceived by someone other than the patient

significant difference \sig nif´i kənt di´fėr əns\ statistical concept indicating that differences noted in data comparison have low probability of occurring randomly

sign language\sīn lang´gwidj\ communication of thoughts or ideas through manual signs and gestures

simian crease\sim´ē ən krēs\ single, transverse palmar crease that is found with increased frequency among Down's syndrome individuals

sinistrality\sin´´is tral´i tē\ lefthandedness

sitomania \sī´´tə mā´nē ə\ excessive craving for food

sitophobia\sī´´tə fō´bē ə\ fear of eating

situationism \si´´chü ā´shə niz´´əm\ the belief that behavior is mostly in response to immediate environmental stimulation

situation psychosis \si´´chü ā´shən sī kō´sis\ reactive disorder

size constancy \sīz kon´stən sē\ seeing the size of an object as remaining the same despite differences in viewing distances

skeletal \skel´ə təl´´\ referring to the bones

skepticism \skep´ti siz´´əm\ attitude of doubt

skill \skil\ degree of excellence in one's performance

skotopia \skə tō´pē ə\ dim light vision

sleeping sickness \slē´ping sik´nəs\ encephalitis

sleepwalking \slēp´wäk ing\ somnambulism

slip of the tongue \slip uv the tung\ inadvertent mistake in speaking believed, in Freudian psychology, to reveal inner conflict

slow learner \slō lėrn´ėr\ term used to refer to children who are educationally retarded; those having low normal intelligence

smallpox \smôl´poks\ type of viral infection; also called variola

Snellen's chart \snel´ənz chärt\ device used to test visual acuity in which

letters, numbers or other symbols are arranged in graded sizes

social action \sō´shəl ak´shən \ collective endeavor; often refers to that action designed to change existing institutions

social adaptation \sō´shəl ə dap tā´shən\ adjusting to society while meeting group needs

social age \sō´shəl āj\ measure of adaptation to social situations

social competence \sō´shəl kom´pə tens\ level of adaptation to environment

social maturity \sō´shəl mə tėr´i tē\ ability to assume personal and social responsibility

social promotion \sō´shəl prə mō´shən\ pupil advancement in grade with his age peers in spite of not having mastered the previous grade's subject matter

social quotient \sō´shəl kwō´shənt\ an expression of social competence gained by $\dfrac{\text{social age}}{\text{chronological age}} \times 100$ = S.Q.

sociodrama \sō´´sē ō dra´mə\ diagnostic and therapeutic technique in which patients are required to dramatize or act out a situation

socioeconomic \so´´sē ō ek´´ə nom´ik\ pertaining to social and economic background

sociogenic \sō´´sē ō jen´ik\ influenced or caused by social forces

sociogram \sō´´sē ə gram´\ diagrammatic illustration of the relationships among individuals within a group

sociological \sō´´si ə loj´i kəl\ referring to those factors that affect the culture of a group

sociometry \sō´´sē om´ə trē\ measurement of social relationships among individuals in a group

sociopath \sō´sē ə path´´\ individual who manifests little regard or responsibility for conforming to standards or mores of the society in which he or she exists

sodomy \sod´ə mē\ bestiality; anal intercourse

soft palate \soft pal´ət\ a fibromuscular, movable fold attached to the posterior margin of the hard palate

somatic \sō mat´ik\ referring to the body or physical condition

somatology \ sō˝mə tol´ə jē\ science that deals with physical characteristics of human beings

somatomegaly \sə mä˝tə meg´ə lē\ gigantism

somatosexual \sə mä˝tə sek´shü əl\ referring to physical characteristics that distinguish between the sexes

somatotype \sə mat´ə tīp\ referring to a particular body build

somnambulism \som nam´bu¨ liz˝əm\ sleepwalking; a condition of habitual sleepwalking

somnipathy \som nip´ə thē\ disorder of sleep

sonic \son´ik\ pertaining to sound

sonic glasses \son´ik glas´əz\ electronic device used by the blind to detect obstacles

sophistry \sof´ i strē\ an argument or method of reasoning that is incorrect though it appears superficially plausible

sophomania \sof˝ə mā´nē ə\ unfounded belief in and preoccupation with the idea that one is wise

soporific \sop˝ə rif´ik\ causing sleepiness; referring to medications that produce sleep

sound \sound\ the detection of vibrations within air or other media by the hearing mechanism

space perception \spās pėr sep´shən\ awareness of the size, distance, position and apparent shape of an object with respect to the observer

squint \skwint\ strabismus; cross-eyed

stammering \stam´ėr ing\ to speak hesitantly or falteringly

standard deviation \stan´dėrd dē˝vē ā´shən\ a dispersional measurement in a frequency distribution that is the root mean square of the deviations of the mean

stapes \stā´pēz\ one of the auditory ossicles; also called the stirrup

statistics \stə tis´tiks\ the science of collecting and evaluating data

status epilepticus \sta´təs ep˝ə lep´ti kəs\ dangerous condition in which epileptic seizures follow in rapid succession

stenosis \stə nō´sis\ narrowing of duct or canal

stereognosis \stăr˝ē og nō´sis\ the ability to detect weight and configuration of an object by handling it

stereopathy \stăr˝ē o´pə thē\ behavior disorder characterized by persistent, repetitious thoughts or actions

stereopsis \stăr˝ē op´sis\ ability to visualize objects in three dimensions; stereoscopic vision

stereoscopic vision \stăr˝e ə skop´ik vizh´ən\ ability to see objects in three dimensions

stereotyped behavior \stăr˝ē ə tīpt˝ bē hāv´yėr\ persistent, repetitive actions or vocalizations that appear senseless or unmotivated

stereotypy \stăr´ē ə tī˝pē\ habitual repetition of meaningless vocalizations or acts

sterile \stăr´əl\ infertile; not capable of producing young

sterilization \stăr˝ə li zā´shən\ process of making a person or an animal incapable of producing young

stigma \stig´mə\ any characteristic peculiar to a condition that aids in the diagnosis or understanding of the condition

Still's disease \ stilz di zēz˝\ fulminating, acute, systemic form of juvenile rheumatoid arthritis

stimulus \stim´yə ləs\ anything that produces a reaction in a receptor

stirrup \stėr´up\ the stapes; small auditory ossicle

strabismus \strə biz´məs\ eye muscle defect in which both eyes cannot fix on the same point, one eye appears to diverge; also called squint

Strauss' syndrome \strous sin´drōm\ symptom complex that includes hyperactivity, impulsiveness, distractibility and perceptual problems suggestive of minimal central nervous system dysfunction accompanied by normal intelligence

streak gonads \strēk gō´nads\ condition in Turner's syndrome in which the ovaries do not develop fully

strephosymbolia \stref´´ə sim bōl´ē ə\ defect of visual perception in which symbols appear reversed

strophocephaly \stro´´fə sef´ə lē\ congenital defect characterized by facial and cerebral distortion and disproportion

structural \struk´chėr əl\ pertaining to tissues of organs of the body

stupor \stü´pėr\ state of lethargy and diminished responsiveness

Sturge-Weber syndrome \stėr´jē web´ėr sin´drōm\ trigeminal cerebral angiomatosis; neurocutaneous syndrome characterized by nevus flammeus, epilepsy and mental retardation

stuttering \stut´ėr ing\ speech defect marked by disfluency and an awareness of the disfluency by either speaker or listener

sty \stī\ inflammation of sebaceous glands of the eyelids due to infection

stye \stī\ sty

subclinical \sub klin´i kəl\ asymptomatic; without observable signs or manifestations of disease or condition

subconscious \sub kon´shəs\ present in the mind beneath awareness

subculture \sub´kul chėr\ a group with distinctive ethnic or social traits that distinguish it from other groups within the total society

subcutaneous \sub´´kū tā´nē əs\ under the skin

subdural hematoma \sub dėr´əl hē´´mə tō´mə\ swelling of the meninges due to the accumulation of blood beneath dura

subjective \sub jek´tiv\ as perceived by one person

sublethal \sub lē´thəl\ less than deadly; almost fatal

sublimation \sub´´lə mā´shən\ mechanism in which frustrated desire is replaced by a substitute activity

subliminal \sub lim´i nəl\ stimulation below the perceptual threshold

submissiveness \sub mis´iv nəs\ subordination of one's own needs and desires to external control or pressure

subnormal intelligence \sub nôr´məl in tel´i jens\ less than average intelligence as measured by psychometric tests

substitution \sub´´sti tü´shən\ articulatory defect of speech in which a correct sound is replaced by another sound

subvocal \sub vō´kəl\ refers to mental formulation of words without saying them

suggestibility \sug jes´´ti bil´i tē\ personality characteristic of being susceptible to the suggestions and ideas of others

suicidal \sü´´i sī´dəl\ tendency toward self-destruction

sui juris \sü´ē jėr´is\ legal term for the capability of managing one's own affairs independently of supervision

superego \sü´´pėr ē´go \conscience

superfemale \sü´pėr fē´māl\ female whose cells contain more than two X chromosomes; also called poly X or triplo X

superintendent \sü´´pėr in ten´dənt\ chief executive officer of an institutin or school district

supermale \sü´pėr māl\ individual possessing a 47 XYY chromosome configuration; tallness, poor coordination and dull normal intelligence are among the reported characteristics

supernumerary \sü´´pėr nü´mə răr´´ē\ being in excess of the usual number, such as in supernumerary fingers or toes

superstition \sü´´pėr sti´shən\ a belief system held without factual evidence of its truth

supination \sü´´pə nā´shən\ turning of the palm of the hand upward

suppression \sə presh´ən\ conscious inhibition of thoughts or desires

suppressor \sə pres´ėr\ gene that nullifies the effect of another gene but has no detectable effect itself

surrogate \sėr´ə gət\ a person who serves as a substitute for a mother, father or other important person in someone's life

susceptibility \sə sep´´ti bil´i tē\ tendency for a particular disease or condition

Sydenham's chorea \sīd´ən hamz kō rē´ə\ chorea minor

symbiosis \sim bī´ə sis\ a close mutual advantage relationship between individuals or species

symbolism \sim´bə liz´´əm\ representation of one ideal or concept for another

symmetry \sim´ə trē\ having equal form or characteristics on both sides

sympathetic ophthalmia \sim´´pə thet´ik of thal´mē ə\ inflammation of one eye usually as a result of perforating trauma to the other eye

symptom \simp´təm\ manifestation or indication of disease or abnormal condition subjectively perceived by the patient

symptomatology \simp´´tə mə tol´ə jē\ systematic study of symptoms; combined symptoms of a disorder

symptosis \simp tō´sis\ atrophy; wasting away

synapsis \si nap´sis\ period in meiosis in which the two members of every pair of homologous chromosomes are in precise and intimate opposition

syndactyly \sin dak´ti lē\ webbing of the fingers and toes; characteristic of Apert's syndrome

syndrome \sin´drōm\ group of symptoms and signs that occur together to form an identifiable condition

synechia \sə nek´ē ə\ adhesion of the iris to the cornea or lens

synemorphic \si´´nə mōr´fik\ refers to behavior that is appropriate for environmental conditions

synergist \sin´ėr jist\ denotes a muscle that contracts with the agonist or principal muscle performing the action in order to potentiate the action

synergy \sin´ėr jē\ coordination

synesthesia \sin´´əs thē´sē ə\ the association of one sensory modality with another, such as associating colors with temperature

syngamy \sin´gə mē\ joining of gametes in fertilization

syngenesis \sin jen´ə sis\ sexual reproduction

synkinesis \sin´´ki nē´sis\ involuntary movement following voluntary one

synomorphy \sī´nə mōr´´fē\ adaption of behavior to a particular environment or social setting

synophthalmia \sīn´´ōf thal´mē ə\ cyclopia; fusion of the two eyes into one

synostosis \sin´´ə stō´sis\ union between bones that ordinarily remain distinct

synovia \si nōv´ē ə\ synovial fluid; a liquid secreted by the synovial membrane that lubricates joints

synovitis \sin´´ə vī´tis\ inflammation of the synovial membrane; a disorder that inhibits articulation of the joints

syntaxis \sin tak´sis\ articulation

syntonic \sin tōn´ik\ stable, normal response to environmental stimulation

syntropy \sin´trə pē\ the correlation of physical characteristics with tendency for a certain condition or disease to develop from another

syphilis \sif´ə lis\ infectious venereal disease caused by the spirochete treponema pallidum which produces wide variety of physical and neurological defects in human beings

syphilology \sif´´ə lol´ə jē\ branch of medical science that deals with the study of syphilis

syphilophobia \sif´´ə lō fō´bē ə\ morbid fear of syphilis

syringomyelocele \si ring´´go mī´ə lō sēl\ projection of a thin, distended portion of the spinal cord through a defect in the spine in spina bifida

systemic \si stem´ik\ referring to or affecting the body as a whole, such as a systemic poison

tabes \tā´bez\ wasting away of the body or a body part

taboo \ta bü´\ a social or cultural prohibition; an act or social custom set aside as being sacred or profane, forbidden for general use

tabula rasa \tab´ū lə rä´sə\ clean slate; the idea that a child's mind is blank at birth and that experience writes or makes its mark on it

tachistoscope \tə kis´tə skōp´´\ apparatus designed to project visual stimuli upon a screen for brief periods of time

tachycardia \tak´´i kär´dē ə\ excessive rapidity of the heart beat

tachylalia \tak´´i lā´lē ə\ rapid speech

tactile \tak´til\ referring to touch

tactile discrimination \tak´til di skrim´´ə nā´shən\ ability to identify objects by touch

tactual \tak´chü əl\ pertaining to touch

talented \tal´ən təd\ natural ability in a particular area or field of endeavor

talipes \tal´ə pēz´´\ congenital malformation of the foot in which it is twisted into an abnormal position

talking book \tôk´ing bùk\ sound recording of a publication used by the blind

tantrum \tan´trəm\ exhibition of temper

tanyphonia \tan´´i fō´nē ə\ abnormally thin voice

tarantism \tär´ən tiz´´əm\ pathological desire to dance

taste buds \tāst budz\ sense receptors in the mouth

tautology \tä tol´ə jē\ redundancy

taxonomy \tak son´ə mē\ classification or information according to a logical or natural order

Tay-Sachs disease \tā-saks di zēz´\ hereditary, progressive, fatal disorder related to faulty lipid metabolism

teachable \tēch´ə bəl\ capable of being taught

technology \tek nol´ə jē\ science involved with mechanical and industrial arts

telebinocular \tel´´ə bī nok´yə lèr\ type of optical device used to test visual perceptual ability

telethon \tel´ə thon\ an extended television program soliciting support for a cause, such as money to combat a particular disorder

teletractor \tel´ə trak´´tèr\ device used for converting sound waves into tactile stimulation for teaching the deaf

telophase \tel´ə fāz\ final phase of cell division

temperament \tem´prə mənt\ tendency to make a certain kind of emotional response

temporal \tem´pèr əl\ referring to time or to the temples on the side of the head

tendon \ten´dən\ cord attaching muscle to bone

teratogen \tăr´ə tə jèn\ something that produces a defect during prenatal life

teratogenesis \tăr´´ə tə jen´ə sis\ the damaging of offspring *in utero*

teratophobia \tăr´´ə tə fō´bē ə\ excessive fear of bearing defective offspring

terminal process \tèr´mə nəl pro´ses\ disease or condition that will cause the death of an organism

terminology \tèr´´mi nol´ə jē\ the language of a discipline or craft

test \test\ any measurement that develops criteria for judgment of achievement, intelligence, potential or other factors

test battery \test bat´èr ē\ grouping of tests that yields a single score

testes \test´ēz\ plural of testis

testicle \test´ik əl\ testis

testing the limits \test´ing thə lim´itz\ behavior designed to elicit punishment or the threat of punishment in order to establish what is acceptable and what is not

testis \tes´tis\ male reproductive gland located in the scrotum

testosterone \tes tos´tə rōn\ male sex hormone

test profile \test prō´fīl\ a chart showing relative strengths and weaknesses as measured by various tests or test sections

test reliability \test rē lī´´ə bil´i tē\ sequential and internal consistency of an evaluative instrument

test validity \test və lid´i tē\ extent to which an evaluative instrument measures what it purports to measure

tetanus \tet´ə nəs\ a disease in which continual muscle contraction and spasms are present

tetraplegia \te´´trə plē´jē ə\ paralysis of all four extremities

thalidomide \thə lid´ə mīd´´\ sedative popularly used during the 1960s until it was discovered to be teratogenic when utilized during pregnancy

thanatophobia \than´´ə tə fō´bē ə\ excessive preoccupation with dying or death

theomania \thē´´ə mā´nē ə\ mental disorder characterized by preoccupation with religion; belief that one is divine

theophobia \thē´´ə fō´bē ə\ morbid preoccupation and fear of divine punishment

therapeutic \thăr´´ə pū´tik\ concerning treatment

therapeutic abortion \thăr´´ə pū´tik ə bôr´shən\ termination of pregnancy to protect the physical or mental health of the mother

therapeutic milieu \thăr´´ə pū´tik mil ū´\ treatment setting that encompasses all aspects of the social and physical environment for the patient's betterment

therapist \thăr´ə pist\ individual skilled in treatment of physical or psychological defects

therapy \thăr´ə pē\ treatment for disease or disability

theriomorphism \thĕr´´i ō môr´fiz əm\ describing humans as animals or subhumans

thermal \thĕr´məl\ referring to heat

thermalgesia \thĕr´´məl jē´zhə\ a condition in which slight warmth causes pain

thermoreceptor \thĕr´´mō rē sep´tĕr\ receptor sensitive to temperature variations

third sex \thĕrd seks\ homosexuality

thoracic cavity \thôr as´ik kav´i tē\ chest; portion of the body between the neck and the abdomen

threshold \thresh´ōld\ point at which a response is elicited

thrombosis \throm bō´sis\ blood clot formation

thwart \thwôrt\ frustrate

thyroid gland \thī´roid gland\ gland that produces thyroxine (T_4) and triiodothyronine (T_3)—iodine compounds necessary for normal growth and development

thyroxine \thī rok´sin\ iodine compound (T_4) produced by the thyroid gland; synthetic production of the compound is used to treat hypothyroidism

tic \tik\ chronic, intermittent twitching of muscles

time out \ tīm out\ procedure in which an individual is isolated from all possible positive reinforcement

time perception \tīm pĕr sep´shən\ how long an event seems to take

timidity \ti mid´i tē\ mild fear

tinnitus \tin´ī tus\ ringing in the ears

tissue \ti´shü\ body structure made of like cells and serving like purpose

toilet training \toi´lət trān´ ing\ learning to control the elimination processes

token economy \tō´kən ə kon´ə me\ behavior modification system in which symbolic rewards such as points, tokens or play money are issued with the knowledge or hope that desirable exchange will eventuate

toluene \tol´ū ēn\ hydrocarbon produced from coal tar that is used in various glues, spray paints and adhesives; known to be a neuropathogen when inhaled excessively

tonaphasia \tōn´´ə fā´zhə\ defective ability to recall familiar melodies

tone \tōn\ quality of sound; the degree of muscular tension

tongue \tung\ the flexible organ at the bottom of the mouth involved in eating, tasting and speaking; a language

tonic \ton´ik\ characterized by muscle tension

tonic clonic stage \ton´ik klon´ik stāj\ the convulsive stage of a grand mal seizure

tonicity \tō nis´i tē\state of muscle tension of a body

tonitrophobia \ton´´i trə fō´bē ə\ excessive fear of thunder

tonometer \tō nom´i tėr\ device for measuring intraocular pressure

tonus \tō´nus\ the constant slight muscular contraction that serves to maintain posture and to facilitate circulation

tool \tül\ a device used to effect environmental changes

topographic \top´´ə graf´ik\ pertaining to a part or region of the body

torpor \tôr´pėr\stupor; lethargy

torticollis \tôr´´ti kol´is\ wryneck; twisted neck resulting in abnormal head position

toxemia \tok sē´mē ə\ condition in which the blood contains toxic or poisonous substances

toxemia of pregnancy \tok sē´mē ə uv preg´nən sē´´\ intoxication due to metabolic disturbances during pregnancy that may damage or kill the fetus

toxic \tok´sik\ poisonous

toxoplasma gondii \tok´´sō plaz´mə gon´dē ī\ protozoan microorganism that causes toxoplasmosis

toxoplasmosis \tok´´sō plaz mō´sis\ infectious disease caused by toxoplasma gondii

trachea \trā´kē ə\ a cylindrical tube from the larynx to the bronchial tube bifurcation

trachoma \tra kō´mə\ viral infection of the eye that causes pain, lacrimation, light sensitivity and visual defect

tract \trakt\ group of similar nerve fibers

train \trān\ teach skills; discipline, instruction

trainability \trān´´ə bil´i tē\ ability to be trained

training school \trā ning skül\ institution emphasizing education and habilitation

trait \trāt\ distinguishing characteristic

trance \trans\ a state of lowered consciousness to external stimuli

tranquilize \tran´kwi līz´´\ to make calm and placid

tranquilizer \tran´kwi lī´zėr\ a drug that calms or sedates

transaction \trans ak´shən\ a psychological happening, one in which certain behaviors and participants are distinguishable

transference \trans´fėr əns\ in psychoanalysis, feeling about the therapist as one felt about an important person in one's life

transient situational personality disorder \ tran´sē ənt sitch´ü ā´shən əl pėr´´sə nal´i tē dis ôr´dėr\ psychological disturbance due to too much environmental pressure

translocation \trans´´lō kā´shən\ in genetics, the attachment of part or all of a chromosome to another chromosome

transmission \ trans mish´ən\ hereditary passing on of a characteristic or characteristics

transplacental \trans´´plə sen´təl\ by means of or through the placenta

transplantation \trans´´plan tā´shən\ the grafting of body tissues either from the same or a different body

transverse \trans´vėrs\ lying, being or moving across

transvestism \trans ves´tiz əm\ the habitual wearing of clothing of the opposite sex

trauma \trä´mə\ injury

treatment \trēt´mənt\ attempt to ameliorate a situation

tremor \trem´ėr\ involuntary, alternate contraction of extensors and flexors that results in a quivering of a body part or parts

treponema pallidum \trep´ə nē´mə pal´i dum\ microorganism that causes syphilis

triad \trī´ad\ a group of three, as of symptoms

trial \tri´əl\ a single attempt; test

trial and error learning \trī´əl and ăr´ér lérn´ ing\ the learning that proceeds from no established pre-conceptions—a number of responses are tried until one is found that brings the desired result

trigeminal cerebral angiomatosis \trī jem´ə nəl sə rē´brəl an´´jē ō mə tō´ sis\ Sturge-Weber syndrome

trimester \trī mes´tér\ three-month period, usually used with respect to pregnancy

triplegia \trī plē´jē ə\ paralytic involve-ment of three extremities

trisome \trī´sōm\ individual possessing an additional chromosome to one of the normal chromosome pairs in his or her karyotype

trisomic \trī sōm´ik\ have three instead of the usual two of a chromosome set

trisomy x \trī sō´mē X\ superfemale, 47 XXX

trisomy 21 \trī sō´mē 21\ Down's syndrome

trophic \trof´ik\ referring to nutrition

truancy \trü´ən sē\ a leave without proper authority, as a child from school

tuberculosis \tü´´bér kū lō´sis\ infec-tious condition caused by Koch's bacillus

tuberous sclerosis \tü´bér əs sklə rō´sis\ neurocutaneous syndrome characterized by epilepsy, adenoma sebaceum and mental retardation

tumescence \tü mes´əns\ swelling

tumor \tü´mér\ neoplasm

tunnel vision \tun´əl vizh´ən\ constric-tion of the visual fields; in psycholo-gy, refers to concentration on a limited area to the exclusion of other environmental stimulation

Turner's syndrome \térn´érs sin´drōm\ 45 XO chromosome disor-der characterized by decreased de-velopment of secondary sex charac-teristics, infertility and possible mental retardation

twitch \twich\ sudden jerk

tympanic membrane \tim pan´ik mem´brān\ eardrum

typify \tip´i fī\ to be an example or symbol

typology \tīp ol´ə jē\ study of types, psychological or otherwise

tyrosine \tī´rə sēn\ amino acid found in protein substances

U **ulceration** \ul´´sə rā´shən\ open sore

ulna \ul´nə\ large bone of the forearm

ultrasonic \ul´´trə son´ik\ beyond what the human ear can hear

ultraviolet \ul´´trə vī´ ə lət\ invisible light

umbilical cord \um bil´i kəl kôrd\ tube that communicates between the placenta and the fetus

unadjustment \un´´ə just´mənt\ not coping; the step preceding maladjustment

unambivalent \un´´am bi´və lənt\ harmonious; not contradictory

unaware need \un ə wăr´ nēd\ a need that cannot be verbalized because of anxiety

unconditioned response \un kon di´shənd ri spons´\ a reaction to a stimulus that is not the result of experience as in the startle reflex to a sudden loud sound

unconscious \un kon´shəs\ insensible; unaware of one's environment; in psychiatry, that part of our personality consisting of complex feelings and drives of which we are unaware and that are not available to our consciousness

underachievement \un´dėr ə chēv´mənt\ achievement at a level significantly below expectations

under age \un´dėr āj´\ younger than other classmates

undifferentiated \un´´dif ėr en´shē āt´´əd\ not set apart from the whole

undoing \un dü´ing\ a defense mechanism designed to erase or wipe out a certain regretted act

undulatory \un´dü lə tôr´´ē\ wave shaped

ungraded class \un grād´əd clas\ a special education grouping

uniaural \ū´´ni ôr´əl\ hearing in one ear

unidextrality \ū´´ni deks tral´i tē\ favoring of one hand in performing tasks

uniformity \ū´´ni fôrm´i tē\ evenness; sameness

unilateral \ū´´ni la´tėr əl\ refers to one side

uninhibited \un´´in hib´i təd\ free from restraint

unique \ū nēk´\ one of a kind

unisexual \ū´´ni sek´shü əl\ referring to only one sex

unison \ū´ni sən\ all together

unit plan \ū´nit plan\ way of organizing teaching in which a large amount of work is based on a common theme

unit teaching \ū´nit tēch´ing\ technique of organizing learning experiences around a central theme

unlearning \un´lėrn ing\ attempt to undo what has been learned previously

unresolved \un´rē zolvd\ not worked out

unsocial \un sō´shəl\ avoidance of social situations

upgrading \up´grād ing\ improvement or promotion

uptight \up´tīt\ (slang) anxious, tense or nervous

uranism \ū´rən iz´´əm\ homosexuality between males

uremia \ū rē´mē ə\ toxic condition related to high level urinary components in the blood

urethra \ū rēth´rə\ duct carrying urine from the bladder

uric acid \ūr´ik as´id\ nitrogen compound found in human urine; hyperuricemia is characteristic of Lesch-Nyhan syndrome and gout

uterus \ū´tėr əs\ hollow organ in the female that houses and nourishes the fetus until birth

utility \ū ti´li tē\ fitness; usefulness

uvea \ū´vē ə\ vascular coat of the eyeball that includes the iris, ciliary body and choroid

uveitis \ū´´vē ī´təs\ inflammation of the uvea

uvula \ū´və lə\ the small fleshy mass descending from the soft palate at the rear of the oral cavity; uvula palatina

V **vaccination** \vak´´si nā´shən\ the injection of a vaccine so as to induce immunity

vaccine \vak´sēn\ weakened or dead solution of microorganisms injected into or taken orally by individuals to induce immunity to a disease

vacuous \vak´ū əs\ empty; devoid of ideas or intelligence

vagina \va jī´nə\ canal from uterus to vulva in the female of the species

vaginism \vaj´i niz´´əm\ painful vaginal spasms often associated with aversion to sexual intercourse

valetudinarian \val´´i tüd´´ə năr´ē ən\ sickly; a person who is overly concerned about poor health

valgus \val´gəs\ refers to position away from the midline of the body

value judgment \val´ū juj´mənt\ decision of worth about a person, place or thing

value system \val´ū sis´təm\ what a person values or deems worthwhile

vandalism \ van´də liz´´əm\ unwarranted destruction of other's property

vanity \van´i tē\ conceit; excessive pride

variability \văr´´ē ə bil´i tē\ unlikeness; change

variable \văr´ē ə bəl\ a value that is subject to change

variola \văr´´ē ō´lə\ smallpox

varus \văr´əs\ refers to position toward the midline of the body

vascular \vas´kū lėr\ pertaining to or full of vessels

vascular occlusion \vas´kū lėr ə klū´zhən\ closing up of a blood vessel or vessels

vas deferens \vas def´ə rənz\ excretory tube of the testes

vasectomy \vas ek´tə mē\ surgical birth control measure in men; cutting or removing part of the vas deferens, the sperm conducting tube

vasomotor \vas´ō mō´´tər\ referring to expansion and contraction of the blood vessels

velleity \və le´ə tē\ weak motivation

velopharyngeal incompetence \vel´´ō fãr´´ in jē´əl in kom´pə təns\ defect of air flow control during speech

velum \vel´um\ the soft palate

venereal \və nēr´ē əl\ related to sexual contact, as with certain diseases

venous \vē´nəs\ referring to the veins

ventilation \vent i lā´shən\ air movement; psychological airing or verbal exposing of problems

ventral \ven´trəl\ referring to the belly or the side of the body that contains the belly

ventricle \ven´tri kəl\ any small cavity

verbal \vėr´bəl\ referring to words

verbal intelligence \vėr´bəl in tel´i jens\ intellectual ability based upon mastery of word concepts

verbalism \vėr´bə liz´´əm\ use of words without understanding their meanings

verbalization \vėr´´bəl i zā´shən\ expressing in words

verbatim \vėr bā´təm\ exact; word for word

verbigeration \vėr´´bij ėr ā´shən\ cataphasia

vergence \vėr´jəns\ eye movement; the turning of one eye

verification \văr´´i fi kā´shən\ checking the correspondence between objective data and an explanation of the facts

vertebra \vėr´tə brə\ one of the thirty-three bones that make up the spinal column

vertex \vėr´teks\ crown of the head

vertigo \vėr´tə gō\ sensation disorder in which an individual feels his surroundings are spinning around him

vesania \ve sā´nē ə\ psychosis; mental disturbance

vesical \ves´i kəl\ referring to the bladder

vesicle \ves´i kəl\ sac that holds liquids

vestigial \ves tij´əl\ in physiology, refers to an organ remnant that remains when the organ has severely undeveloped due to teratogenesis

viability \vī ə bil´i tē\ potential or capacity to live, develop or exist

viable \vī´ə bəl\ capable of living, developing or existing

vicarious \vī kăr´ē əs\ referring to substitute

vicarious reinforcement \vī kăr´ē əs rē´´in fors´mənt\ process of strengthening a response through observing others being rewarded for the response

virulent \vēr´ū lənt\ poisonous; dangerous

viscera \vis´ėr ə\ plural of viscus; large internal organs

visceral \vis´ėr əl\ referring to the viscera

vision \vizh´ən\ sight; the faculty of seeing

visual acuity \vizh´ū əl ə kū´i tē\ ability to see clearly

visual adaptation \vizh´ū əl ə dap tā´shən\ change in visual sensitivity

visual aphasia \vizh´ū əl ə fā´zhə\ inability to make sense of writing

visual field \vizh´ū əl fēld\ that scene perceivable to a stationary pair of eyes

visual handicap \vizh´ū əl han´dē kap´´\ partial loss of visual function

visualization \vizh´´ ū ə lī zā´ shən\ imagery within the mind in the absence of external ocular stimulation

visual memory \vizh´ū əl mem´ə rē\ the ability to recall accurately what was previously seen

vital \vī´təl\ referring to life

vital capacity \vī təl kə pas´i tē\ the greatest amount of air that can be exhaled after maximum inhalation

vital function \vī´təl fungk´shən\ any bodily process necessary to life

vitamin \vī´tə min\ term for a number of organic substances necessary for normal metabolic functioning of the body

vitiation \vi´´shē ā´shən\ impairment of quality, injury or contamination of use or efficiency

vitiligo \vit ə lī´go\ white patches of the skin caused by depigmentation

vitreous humor \vi´trē əs hū´mėr\ material the consistency of jelly filling the eyeball

vitreous opacities \vi´trē əs ō pas´ə tēz´´\ floaters in the eye that interfere with vision

vocal \vō´kəl\ referring to voice

vocal cords \vō´kəl kôrdz\ organs of sounds; the ligaments in the throat that vibrate to produce voice

vocalization \vō´´kəl ī zā´shən\ communicating by means of sounds

vocal organs \vō´kəl ôr´ganz\ anything and everything used in the production of speech

vocation \vō kā´shən\ life work

vocational counseling \vō kā´shən əl koun´sə ling\ guidance in choosing and preparing for a vocation

volar \vō´lėr\ referring to the bottom surfaces of hand or foot

volition \vō li´shən\ voluntary initiation of action

voluntary muscle \vol´´ən tăr´ē mus´əl\ one that can be contracted at will

von Recklinghausen's disease \von´rek´´ling hou´zəns di zēz´\ neurofibromatosis

voyeur \voi´yėr\ one who derives sexual gratification from seeing the sexual activity of others

voyeurism \voi´´yėr iz´əm\ sexual gratification through observation of others

vulva \vul´və\ the external female genitalia

W **Waardenburg's syndrome** \wôr´dən bergz´´ sin´drōm\ a developmental defect characterized by heterochromia, white forelock, large mandible and occasional mental retardation

walleyed \wäl´īd\ colloquial for divergent strabismus

Wasserman test \wäs´ er mən test\ test for syphilis

waterhead \wä´ter hed´\ colloquialism for hydrocephalus

weaning \wēn ing\ in psychology, the breaking of unwanted dependencies

well adjusted \wel ə just´əd\ referring to a healthy manner of dealing with one's environment

whooping cough \hü´ping kôf\ infectious respiratory disease; pertussis

will \wil\ volition; capacity for voluntary action

willfulness \wil´ful nəs\ a compulsion to get one's way regardless of the consequences

Wilson's disease \wil´səns di zēz´\ hereditary copper metabolism disorder characterized by hepatolenticular degeneration, tremors, drooling, fixed facial expression and gradual intellectual decline

wish \wish\ longing for something without taking action to acquire it

wish fulfillment \wish ful fil´mənt\ indirect satisfaction of a desire through imaginary gratification

withdrawal \with drô´əl\ avoidance of a situation; reduction or stoppage of addictive drugs; coitus interruptus

withdrawal symptoms \with drô əl simp´təms\ physical responses of an addict when drug usage is curtailed

withdrawn behavior \with drôn´ bē hāv´yer\ that in which low affect is evidenced in social relationships

wit work \wit werk\ unconscious psychological mechanism that produces wit

womb \wümb\ the uterus of the human female

word blindness \werd blīnd´nəs\ alexia

word configuration \werd kən fig´´ū rā´shən\ visual pattern of a word on the printed page

word deafness \werd def´nəs\ auditory aphasia

world view \werld vū\ way of perceiving and explaining reality

wristdrop \rist´drop\ hand disorder due to paralysis of extensor muscles of hand and fingers

wryneck \rī´nek\ torticollis; twisted neck

116

X

x-axis \eks-ak´sis\ the abscissa; the horizontal plane in a Cartesian coordinate system

x-chromosome \eks krō´mə sōm\ the sex chromosome that carries the genetic direction for femaleness that normally occurs in pairs in females and singly in males

xenoglossophilia \zen´´ō glos´´ə fil´ē ə\ use of strange and complicated words instead of familiar, comfortable ones

xenoglossophobia \zen´´ō glos´´ə fō´bē ə\ pathological fear of foreign languages

xenophobia \zen´´ə fō´ bē ə\ excessive fear of strangers or foreigners

xenophonia \zen´´ə fō´nē ə\ drastic change in the accent or intonation of a person's speech

xerosis \zə rō´sis\ abnormal dryness of the skin or eye

x-linked gene \eks´-lingkt jēn\ gene located in the X chromosome

x ray \eks´ rā\ roentgen ray

Y

y-axis \wī-ak´sis\ the ordinate; the vertical plane in a Cartesian coordinate system

yellow-sighted \yel´ō-sīt´əd\ visual sensitivity to yellow coloration

yerkish \yér´kish\ communication system utilizing a symbol board that was developed to communicate with chimpanzees and has also been used with the severely retarded

youth \yūth\ adolescent; juvenile

Z

zelotypia \zel´´ə tīp´ē ə\ insane jealousy; abnormal zeal or dedication

zest \zest\ healthy interest in life

zonules \zōn´ūls\ fine ligaments that hold the lens of the eye in place

zoolagnia \zō´´ə lag´nē ə\ sexual interest in animals

zoophilia \zō´´ə fīl´ē ə\ abnormal affection for animals or a particular animal; zoomania

zoophobia \zō´´ə fō´bē ə\ irrational fear of animals

zygosis \zī gō´sis\ the union of sperm and egg

zygote \zī´gōt\ fertilized egg

117